Church growth is more than an increase in the number of people who attend weekly. It's measured by the ministry of church members, the impact of the church on the surrounding community, and the church's ability to reproduce daughter churches. Robert Logan guides you in developing an effective philosophy for stimulating church growth. This comprehensive guide presents ten key principles:

- Visionizing Faith and Prayer
- Effective Pastoral Leadership
- Culturally Relevant Philosophy of Ministry
- Celebrative and Reflective Worship
- Holistic Disciple Making
- Expanding Network of Cell Groups
- Developing and Resourcing Leaders
- Mobilizing Believers According to Spiritual Gifts
- Appropriate and Productive Programming
- Starting Churches That Reproduce

Outlining the steps required to meet defined goals, Dr. Logan points out possible trouble areas and offers solutions. You will find the help you need to increase your church's ministries within your walls...to your neighbors ...and to the ends of the earth in *Beyond Church Growth*.

Beyond

CHURCH
GROWTH

BY Robert E. Logan:
   Leading and Managing Your Church (with Carl F. George)
   Beyond Church Growth

Beyond
CHURCH GROWTH

ROBERT E. LOGAN

Fleming H. Revell Company
Tarrytown, New York

Library of Congress Cataloging-in-Publication Data

Logan, Robert E.
   Beyond church growth / Robert E. Logan.
     p. cm.
   ISBN 0-8007-5332-1
   1. Church growth. I. Title.
BV652.25.L64 1989
254′.5—dc20   89-30490
                                  CIP

TO Carl George, a mentor and friend who has stimulated and encouraged me toward greater effectiveness in ministry

Contents

Preface

. . . on this rock I will build my church, and the gates of Hades will not overcome it.

Matthew 16:18

My earliest memories are of church—sitting between my parents, making an attempt to keep up with the hymn singing, at times attentive, at times doodling on the bulletin or whispering questions to my mom and dad.

Someone watching from his pew in our staunchly evangelical Baptist church in Santa Monica, California, would have seen nothing more than a fidgety five-year-old boy who couldn't wait to be released to chase pigeons in the hazy California sunshine.

Yet the river into which these tributaries of Sunday-morning worship flowed ran far deeper in my soul. I still can close my eyes and sense God's infinite Being in that place, sense his brooding over the waters, a deep quietness behind which—to a child's intent inner ear—the presence of God patiently waited.

I suppose I worshiped him, as children do, with the joy and freedom that is theirs uniquely. Only a child can jump upon the lap of God without fear or guilt. Jesus said, ". . . the kingdom of heaven belongs to such as these" (Matthew 19:14). The remainder of our lives seems an arduous struggle to return to that place where we can release ourselves unreservedly into his embrace.

The sense of God's calling on my life strengthened with each passing year. Before I was eight, I had asked Jesus Christ to cleanse my sins, come live in my heart, and make me a member of his family forever. Yet I knew there was more. I knew that God wanted me to work for him, so I committed myself to full-time missionary service.

This goal was ever before me as I progressed through school. I earned a degree in chemistry from UCLA and seriously considered pursuing medical missions. But God steered me differently during my junior year of college, and instead I entered Western Conservative Baptist Seminary and began studying for the pastorate.

Most of Western's graduates sought pulpit assignments in traditional church settings. But not me. In 1977 with my master of divinity degree in hand, I somehow ended up on the hilly streets in the rapidly growing suburban community of Alta Loma. I had no apparent prospects for employing my newly acquired skills. Yet I was intrigued with the thought of starting a church—building a church which satisfied my own peculiar ideas of what a church should be.

It sounded like a great idea to my young wife, Janet, and me. Perhaps I would have continued coolly through that process had it not been for the malicious designs of that most pernicious of all bubble bursters—reality. I spent two months knocking on doors, trying to generate interest, and trying to figure out what to do next, when it hit me: *I didn't know what in God's name I was doing!*

The Dream

That night, out of my utter despair, I had a vision—Well, best not to call it a vision if you've graduated from a Conservative Baptist seminary. Let's call it a dream—a nightmare, really.

I was watching thousands upon thousands of church planters standing on the seashore. Someone (I think it was God) spoke in a loud voice: "Okay, everyone, listen up! Your objective—swim to Catalina Island. Line up, and start at my signal!"

The starter's pistol fired, and the bewildered church planters jockeyed for position as the waves pounded at their feet. A few hearty souls splashed and floundered. Some sank immediately. Most began to wade gingerly into the waves, longingly glancing back at the shore. Their objective lay shrouded in ocean mists, some twenty-seven near-impossible miles distant.

As I observed the events that followed, I began asking God questions. Seeing one church planter after another pulled into the same undercurrent, I blurted out, "Why aren't there buoys to warn church planters and pastors of hazards to avoid during the swim?" Everyone seemed to be making the same fatal mistakes over and over again! Then I saw one unlucky swimmer sink under the water for the third time. He didn't come up again. "Why aren't there lifeboats to rescue those who are going under?" I cried. When I realized this wasn't the first such group in history to launch upon those waters, I angrily wondered, "Where are the church planters who have completed the swim successfully in the past? Why aren't they returning to tell us how to do it?"

The Reality

In those subsequent, miserable days, the reality of my dilemma engulfed me. My seminary education didn't prepare me for 80 percent of what I now was attempting to do.

I had been a very good student. I had learned how to study the Bible, how to interpret and analyze it, and to a lesser extent how to teach or preach it in a relatively effective manner. Although these were valuable skills, they had little bearing on the task of building a church. I felt as if I had secured a very specialized job in electrical engineering after earning my degree in chemistry.

In spite of my nagging frustration, I somehow sensed that God had brought me this far for a purpose. Perhaps he had granted me the church-planting dream.

So I got on my knees, and from the depths of my heart I cried out to God for help: "Lord, I'm not sure what I'm doing here, but I think you have brought me to this moment. I don't have the faintest notion how to accomplish the idea you've put into my head. But you *have* put something there, an ideal, a vision of what your Church ought to look like.

"Until now, Lord, I have considered myself to be the builder of this church. But from now on I recognize and confess that *you are the Builder of your Church.* Please show me what you want me to do."

After further pondering my dream of the seashore, I added, "Lord, we're not learning from the successes or failures of other church planters. I promise you this: When you get me out of this mess, and if you ever place me in the position to help the others lined up on the shore, that's what I want to do."

The Beginning

I realized that I needed help. My first step was to gather all the available materials relating to church growth and church planting. I accumulated a very small armful and began reading.

With great disappointment, I discovered that everything I read fell into one of two categories, neither of which was very helpful to my situation. Some books were full of helpful principles, but did not explain how to apply them. They were theoretical and not practical.

Other books discussed specific church-planting or church-growth methods, but their models were so tailored to reach their specific target groups that I knew they would not work if I applied them in my own unique situation. By God's grace these authors somehow had built successful churches in their own context, but duplicating their methods in a different context would only lead to disaster.

My own church planting proceeded primarily on the basis of trial and error. Due to God's grace and mercy, a thriving network of churches is now in place, in spite of my mistakes. The mother church I planted became Community Baptist Church (affectionately known as "CBC") of Alta Loma. During the eleven years that I served as pastor, it grew to a worship attendance of more than 1,200 people, many of whom previously were unchurched. CBC offers five weekly worship services to accommodate the crowds.

Between 1984 and 1988 CBC planted six daughter churches in surrounding communities. Because these daughter churches are established with goals of growing, ministering, and planting new churches, the future for growth is bright for this network of churches, which is reaching out and expanding God's kingdom in suburban Los Angeles communities and beyond.

Much of my work in this process has required something equivalent to reinventing the wheel. Very little guidance is available for a pastor who truly desires to do what God intends churches to do. The Charles E. Fuller Institute of Evangelism and Church Growth, based in Pasadena, California, was of great assistance to me in this process. The information presented to you in this book I have learned primarily in the crucible of life's experiences, by trial and error.

I was fortunate that, in spite of my lack of experience, God still allowed me to start a healthy, growing church. Since planting CBC I have met many pastors whose early church-planting starts miscarried simply because the cost of reinventing the wheel was too high.

An exciting aspect of being part of a dynamic, growing local church body is seeing God weave together people's gifts and passions to accomplish his purpose. Sometimes his purpose is a total surprise. During a staff prayer time in January 1987, a woman who on several occasions had spoken a prophetic word which later was proven to be from the Lord, told me, "Bob, the Lord is releasing you from the pastorate."

Needless to say, this unnerved me. I was thoroughly enjoying my work with the church, and felt that we were on the verge of an explosion of growth and ministry. I loved CBC and I knew that God was going to take her wonderful places. With all my heart I wanted to stick around and see that happen!

Because the Lord recently had given me a specific agenda for my ministry at CBC over the next eighteen to twenty-four months, I focused my attention on the task at hand and prayerfully waited for further clarification and confirmation.

Ten months later, my wife, Janet, took me to lunch and confirmed this by asking me whether the activities I was involved in were satisfying the assignment God was giving me. As usual, she knew more about what was happening in my heart than I did.

Upon reflection, I realized that my spirit did feel a growing sense of restlessness. The activities which my role as a pastor demanded no longer were those that satisfied me. I was becoming increasingly concerned about my role in the larger body of Christ, about the task of raising up and equipping church planters, and about seeing new churches extend Christ's kingdom into the far corners of the globe. I realized the itch wasn't being scratched in quite the right place yet.

My lack of peace about these issues drove me to consider how I might restructure my role with CBC in order to free me from many of my pastoral duties and allow me to spend more time in my church-planting work. Janet and I met with a close friend and associate, Jim Dethmer, a dynamic church planter and pastor of Grace Fellowship Church in Baltimore. Jim made me realize that I desired to do task-oriented activities that would be fulfilled only through my involvement in a missions organization and not through my role as a church pastor. He then directed me to Church Resource Ministries (CRM), a young but creative missions organization in Fullerton, California. Through interacting with CRM we realized that God had prepared a place there for me to do the tasks he was putting in my heart.

It is extremely difficult to leave a church you have founded, particularly at such a window of opportunity. But God clearly was calling me to CRM, and I turned the leadership of CBC over to my longtime friend and colleague, Dr. Robert Acker.

My father is a godly man who had a tremendous impact on my life. Over the years he told me many times, "True success is finding out what God wants you to do—and doing it." Sometimes the cost of obedience seems overwhelming, yet its rewards are always far greater.

Although what God asks us to do isn't always easy, there always is great reward attached. In my short sojourn with CRM, I have begun to see a glimpse of what God intends to do in his Church on this planet and how my own God-given gifts and passion will play a part as I serve as vice-president for New Church Development with CRM. CBC is now flourishing under Rob Acker's direction—which shouldn't be surprising when God is at work.

Because my task of resourcing church planters very often takes me to foreign shores, I am grateful to God for bringing me full circle to those childhood days when I committed myself to serving him as a missionary.

The same circle also has returned me to that shore where those young pastors and church planters stand poised for their perilous swim. I remember my promise to God and would like to give as much guidance as possible for that journey.

Acknowledgments

I appreciate the team of people who have worked with me in the production of this book. Larry Short invested hours interviewing pastors, church planners, and missionaries as a part of the research process. He also utilized his creativity to transform my working outlines and notes into an excellent first draft of the manuscript. Without his involvement, this book would not have been possible.

Many people have influenced my understanding of church ministry. Special thanks to Robert Acker and Byron Spradlin, who colabored with me to develop these principles and implement them at Community Baptist Church. For over five years, we invested two days a month in a retreat setting to seek God's direction for our lives and work. Many of the things that the Lord taught us during these times of prayer and planning are reflected in this book.

Joan Florio continues to serve faithfully as my secretary. In the midst of a myriad of projects, her encouraging spirit and attention to details provide an essential contribution to the team.

My wife, Janet, inspires me to cultivate godly character through her example of devotion to the Lord. Her faithful prayers and partnership in ministry are constant sources of strength to me.

Introduction

For many years I have been fully committed to the church growth movement—and still am. So why am I writing a book with the title *Beyond Church Growth*? I hope to reach two audiences through this book.

Those Suspicious of Church Growth

First, many pastors and Christian leaders who have rejected church-growth thinking. If you find yourself in that camp, you probably picked up this book thinking, "Finally, something that moves us beyond church growth." As you read, you'll probably appreciate the focus on church health. *Beyond Church Growth* will help your church become more effective in ministry. Effective churches are healthy churches; healthy churches are growing churches—they make more and better disciples. This is precisely the focus of the church-growth movement. So if the title gets more pastors and Christian leaders to take a fresh look at the process of all that is involved in making more and better disciples, then one of my objectives for writing this book will be realized.

Those Who Fully Embrace Church Growth

Second, many leaders fully committed to the church-growth movement need to expand their ministry horizons. So many pastors and church planters I talk with focus almost exclusively on growing their own local churches and functionally ignore the imperative to start more congregations. To be sure, church planting "sometime in the future" is mentioned, but there is a danger of saying the right thing, but never doing it. Many church-growth pastors should begin making plans to start a daughter church *now*—not next year. Now is the time to establish growing and reproducing churches—both local and global, cross-cultural and mono-cultural, upper class and lower class. The harvest is ripening—we need to go forth. That's the second reason for the title *Beyond Church Growth*. It's time to move beyond the church growth to active involvement in church planting.

The Task

More than ever, I am convinced that church planters deserve to be—but are not adequately equipped for—the task of planting

churches. Likewise, pastors who lead existing churches are not adequately equipped for their role by their education. Even lay leaders
could benefit from specific training in church growth and ministry.

It is inarguable that God will fulfill his objective on this planet—the
harvesting of disciples—through his churches. God makes no other
promises that anything else will "prevail against the gates of hell" (see
Matthew 16:18). I desire to do everything in my power to equip men
and women to build more and better churches, which in turn can make
more and better disciples.

We can better understand the task of building more and better
churches by examining the following three assumptions.

Church

The universal Church is God's agent of change on this planet; the
local church is his plan for developing his kingdom in the lives of
believers. If our service is to be of value to God, it must promote, uplift,
and strengthen both the universal Church and the local church. The
church also has a valid expression in numerous, task-oriented mission
organizations. These help extend the Church universal, when they
work in tandem with the church in its local expression.

Growth

God desires that churches grow both qualitatively and quantitatively
so that the Gospel of the kingdom will spread to the uttermost ends of
the earth in fulfillment of the Great Commission. Lasting church
growth flows out of church health. Healthy churches make obedient
disciples and start new churches.

Intentional

Even in the best of churches, health that produces growth is not
natural in the sense that it is spontaneous or automatic. It carefully
must be planned for, nurtured, worked hard for, monitored, and ex-
ploited.

In reality, these are not so much assumptions as they are facts. There
is strong scriptural, historical, and statistical support for all three
tenets, but I am labeling them assumptions because it would be worthless for you to proceed further in this book if you did not share these
tenets with me. If you are not committed to both the universal Church
and the local church; if you are leading a "comfortable" church with no

desire to rise to the occasion and challenge your people to God-honoring growth; if you aren't willing to do the planning and work required to make this growth a reality; if you aren't willing to realize that your brain and muscles are among the instruments God will use to accomplish his purposes then I politely dismiss you to your own devices. The rest of us then can roll up our sleeves and get to work.

The Process

Through my own trial-and-error process of leading churches to growth, I have discovered several truths the Christian leader must understand.

First, God's principles never change. They are not bound by time or culture. However, the application of these changeless principles will be different in every ministry context. For example, one of these principles, as we will discuss later, is that God has designed churches as living organisms which must be involved in the process of creating new churches in order to be healthy and to fulfill his plan. They can reproduce churches through a variety of methods, each of which is applicable in a different situation.

Second, pastors and church leaders need a well-defined process to help structure prayerful thought so the Holy Spirit can guide them to the appropriate application of principles for their unique situation.

This book presents ten of God's principles crucial to the health of growing churches. It also outlines in detail how leaders can receive the Holy Spirit's guidance to arrive at the appropriate application of these principles for their church.

The Principles

This book devotes one chapter to each of the following ten church-growth principles:

- Visionizing Faith and Prayer
- Effective Pastoral Leadership
- Culturally Relevant Philosophy of Ministry
- Celebrative and Reflective Worship
- Holistic Disciple Making
- Expanding Network of Cell Groups
- Developing and Resourcing Leaders
- Mobilizing Believers According to Spiritual Gifts
- Appropriate and Productive Programming
- Starting Churches That Reproduce

When appropriately applied to specific situations, these ten principles have proven equally applicable across urban/rural, ethnic, cross-cultural, or socioeconomic boundaries. Each principle first is explained, then illustrated in a variety of different settings. Along the way you'll find checklists to narrow the application to your own situation and monitor your progress. Prayerfully seek guidance from the Holy Spirit as you apply these principles. As a result of this process, you may choose to adapt models that have worked in a situation similar to your own, with only minor modifications, or you may choose to forge your own models to apply these principles in your church. In either case, you will find this material most valuable if you carefully follow the specific action steps to help you apply each principle in your own ministry context.

Beyond
CHURCH
GROWTH

Principle 1

Visionizing
Faith and
Prayer

Now to him who is able to do immeasurably more than all we ask or imagine, according to his power that is at work within us, to him be glory in the church and in Christ Jesus throughout all generations, for ever and ever! Amen.

Ephesians 3:20, 21

One of my most important questions to ask pastors and church leaders is: If you knew that you *could not fail,* what would you do for the glory of God and the growth of his kingdom?

A person's answer to this question might be the cup which either enables or limits his ability to receive God's blessing. To the person who holds out a small cup, God may desire to pour out a large blessing, but that person will be able to hold only a very small part of it. The rest may spill over onto someone else, and the one for whom the blessing was intended will miss out, simply because the "cup" of his or her vision was too small to hold God's desires for that person. But if a person holds out a larger cup, when and if God pours out a large blessing, that individual will be able to catch and hold more of it.

If we take seriously the message of Ephesians 3, here's the exciting news: Our cup never can be too large to contain the blessing that God is *able* to pour out upon us. The promise is that God "is able to do *immeasurably more* than all we ask or imagine."

God considers our capacity to imagine his blessing a personal challenge which he desires to meet. Why? As A. W. Tozer asserted, God is transcendent; his true greatness always will be greater than we have the ability to think, believe, or know.

How much is God able to do for us?

It would be quite a revolutionary shift in our thinking, and doubtless in our lives, if we simply were to believe that God was able to do precisely what we ask. Over and over throughout Scripture, we are beseeched to ask of God. James 4:2 assures us, ". . . You do not have, because you do not ask God."

Though our believing that simple truth would be sufficient to radically alter history, the Apostle Paul considered God's desire and ability to bless us and went beyond what we *ask* to what we have the capacity to *imagine*. Isn't it true that most of us can imagine far more than we dare ask?

But he doesn't stop even there. Not only can God do what we ask, or what we imagine, but he also can do *more* than what we ask or imagine. Right? Yes and no. Paul wanted to be so sure that we got the point here that he added a final superlative. God is able to do *immeasurably more* than we ask or imagine!

The question we must ask, then, is not "How much is God able to do?" but rather "How much are we able to imagine?"

Obviously, God does not call us to live in a fantasy world or to be pie-in-the-sky dreamers. And nowhere does Scripture assure us that God is the unqualified granter of every request laid before him. Immediately after writing, "You do not have, because you do not ask God," James adds, "when you ask, you do not receive, because you ask with wrong motives, that you may spend what you get on your pleasures" (James 4:3). Clearly, our requests of God must not be rooted in selfish desire, but must be motivated by a selfless desire to see God glorified. How much of what we can ask or imagine, how much of our vision, is deeply rooted in some self-centered desire—for riches, fame, glory, or even perhaps the seemingly simple desire to be liked by others?

As in the progression of Ephesians 3:20, 21, the nature of "vision" progresses beyond our ability to ask toward our ability to imagine what God is able to do with our lives and our churches.

We might define *vision* as "the ability to see things which are not." At least, things which are not—yet. One day in 1980, Dr. Rick Warren, founding pastor of Saddleback Valley Community Church in Mission Viejo, California, began walking through the streets of this up-and-coming Orange County community. As he saw its people, he began to visualize the type of ministry required to reach them and to meet their needs. He began to visualize a very specific church. He saw 25,000 members. He imagined a church with a worship style and programs to reach "Saddleback Sam," the typical unchurched person in his area.

Warren kept returning to that vision, never letting go of it. He reiterated it to his associates and to the members of his new church. He taught it at the new membership class and preached it from the pulpit. Now with almost 4,000 attenders and listed among the fastest-growing young churches in the United States, Saddleback Valley Community Church is well established on the road to achieving that vision. And the church leadership still communicates that vision at all levels of the church's life.

True vision dismisses for a time the unreality which plagues our everyday lives and replaces it with a peek at the reality that, from God's most realistic viewpoint, already is accomplished.

Elisha had developed a very bad reputation with the king of Aram, who was tired of the prophet's broadcasting his secret battle strategy to the king of Israel. So the king of Aram sent a strong force containing horses and chariots to surround the town of Dothan, where Elisha was staying (2 Kings 6:8–18).

In the morning, Elisha's servant arose and saw the army surrounding them. He ran in and cried out to Elisha in a panic, "Oh, my lord, what shall we do?" (v. 15).

"Don't be afraid," Elisha answered. "Those who are with us are more than those who are with them" (v. 16).

Reality as defined by what the servant could hear, see, smell, and taste at the moment must have convinced him that Elisha finally had flipped. But in the next verse Elisha prayed, "Lord, open his eyes so he may see." And, sure enough, the servant looked up and saw that the Arameans were vastly outnumbered by the multitudinous chariots of fire which breathed godly vapors down their uncomprehending necks.

We would explain this incident by suggesting that the servant had a vision. But the servant would say, "For a moment there I saw reality."

Steps to Achieving Vision

Two steps crucial to achieving vision are unbinding prayer and exposure to need or opportunity.

Unbinding Prayer

Elisha's prayer was a simple one, yet it conformed closely to a New Testament view of our intended role in prayer: "O Lord, open his eyes so he may see." The eyes of every person are bound earthward. All that we perceive to be true is unreal in the sense that it is filtered through physical senses which tell us only partial truth about the absolute nature of our world.

Christ told Peter and the disciples gathered with him, "I will give you the keys of the kingdom of heaven; . . . whatever you loose on earth will be loosed in heaven" (Matthew 16:19).

It's exciting to realize God has granted us the authority to open human eyes so that they may perceive the absolute reality of heavenly truth. Praying for vision is praying for a telescope through which our eyes, unbound by God's authority, may gaze upon heaven, where the unbinding is accomplished in tandem.

Unbinding prayer is a crucial element. Pray, by the authority of Jesus Christ, that your eyes may be opened to see the reality of heaven through the vision that God desires to give you. Ask that the vision be specific and clear.

Dieter Zander, pastor of one of CBC's daughter churches, was driving one day and praying that God would "open his eyes" in this manner. He had considered planting a church, but had no specific ideas. Suddenly, as Dieter was passing through an intersection, his "unbinding" started. He found himself standing in the back of an auditorium, gazing upon a young man preaching before a packed collegiate audience. He was shocked to realize that the man was himself.

He looked around the room, noted the type of people who filled it, got a sense of the environment, the excitement, and the anticipation, and even noticed the color of carpet, the wall hangings, and so on. Then, as quickly as it had begun, the vision was over. He was still passing through the intersection. If any time had elapsed, it was the merest fraction of a second. Dieter is convinced that what he had seen was reality.

Through the details of his vision he began filtering the puzzle pieces which were coming together to form his church. He originally had thought he would fill the church with punk rockers and other down-and-out people. In his vision Dieter says, "I saw that the people of this church were primarily people very much like myself, culturally speaking, and I realized that my desire to fill the church with these other types of people originated primarily in my ego—in my flesh."

Dieter recently moved his rapidly growing church from the junior high school building they had been renting to a more spacious university student-union facility. I asked him if the auditorium there matched that from his vision. "No," he responded, "it didn't. We're not there yet. So I know we have at least one more move to go."

I readily will confess that I never had such a specific vision when I was planting CBC. But just before we met Dieter, Janet and I did have a "vision" in the sense that we had very clear direction from the Lord that he desired us to plant a daughter church designed to reach college students. We prayed that God would raise up this type of church. When Dieter told me about his vision, I knew that God had answered our prayers.

Exposure to Need or Opportunity

This "unbinding" process can be described in many ways. Frank Tillapaugh, pastor of Bear Valley Baptist Church in Denver, calls it "unleashing" a person's potential. The second step in ascertaining vision, *exposure to need*, is well illustrated by the way God gave Frank and his church the vision for their tremendous ministries.

One of the most powerful influences on Frank's vision for ministry resulted from his tenure at Long Beach State University in Southern California during the era of student unrest and radical movements. Frank dug beneath the students' angry rhetoric and realized that what these people longed for and demanded was more closely akin to the reality of the New Testament church than any other sociological structure. Frank caught a God-given vision that people needed holistic ministry, that Christ holds us accountable to exercise mercy and justice and to minister to the physical needs of hurting people as well as to their spiritual needs.

It was this realization—this vision—that helped shape a plethora of people ministries which have sprung from Bear Valley Baptist Church. A coffeehouse, medical clinic, ministry to unwed mothers, and several dozen more outreaches touch the lives of nearly eight thousand hurting people in the Denver area each month. Frank says that the people of Bear Valley Baptist Church are just beginning to experience the reality of what those radical students of the sixties were seeking.

Studying the people around us—the people for whom Christ died—plays an important role in forming pastoral vision. The ministry of Christ himself was at least in part defined by his compassion for the lost sheep around him. Matthew reports, "When he saw the crowds, he had compassion on them, because they were harassed and helpless, like sheep without a shepherd. Then he said to his disciples, 'The harvest is plentiful but the workers are few' " (Matthew 9:36, 37).

We so often lift the latter part of this section from its context and speak simply of the need to pray for workers. We do need to pray for workers, but it's fascinating to see that the event which gave rise to this principle was the compassion Christ felt as a result of his exposure to and observation of lost people. To feel compassion, to "have our hearts broken by the things which break the heart of God," is to allow God-given vision for ministry to enrich and empower us at the very first level. This will spring only from both prayer and exposure to human needs.

There was a time at Bear Valley Baptist when Frank alone had a vision for and cared deeply enough about people's needs to take action. But that soon changed. During a Sunday-morning worship service, he asked the congregation to stand. They were prepared to sing another hymn or to bow in prayer, but they weren't prepared to be asked to leave the auditorium and to load into waiting buses!

The buses wheeled them to a downtown section of Denver, where homeless and hurting people were seen on every street corner and in every back alley. They got out of the buses and walked the streets. For many of these Denver residents, it was the first time they ever had come face-to-face with hurting and homeless people. After a time, the guided tour was over, and Frank's congregation filed back into the buses, which returned them to the church. For the most part, the crowd was silent. Several remarked that the experience was the most powerful sermon they ever had heard at Bear Valley.

In a compassionate heart softened and prepared by God's Spirit, exposure to people's needs gives birth to godly vision for ministry. Do you wish to establish a church, or are you serving in a church? First, walk the streets of the community. See its people. Talk with them and ask them what their needs are. Then pray that God would open your eyes to see the reality of what type of ministry, by the power of his Holy Spirit, God would give through you to meet the needs of those hurting people. The opportunities are limitless!

A Well-Kept Secret

It is God's nature to bless his people. This is a simple statement, but do we truly believe it? God has chosen to work through his people to accomplish his purposes. Rarely does he send angels when an ordinary human being will do. Rather than causing Goliath to trip over an exposed root and run himself through with his own sword, which would have been easy for God to do, he sent a courageous, faithful young boy named David to employ his slingshot skills to bring down the boastful giant. God loves, when he can, to work through people.

Why is this such a well-kept secret? Ever since Eve met the serpent at the tree in the garden, we've bought in to the line that God is trying to hold us back from becoming everything that we could be, or that he has something very unpleasant in store for us. Scripture reveals the opposite to be true.

First Chronicles records the brief story of a fellow who got a very rough start in life. His mother had a lot of trouble in childbirth, and so, perhaps without much foresight, named her child *Jabez*, which translated means "pain." Someone named *Pain* probably would have a deflated self-esteem and a good excuse for moping around and complaining, "God is setting me up to fail. No way am I going to do anything *he* wants."

Yet learn from how Jabez handled his problems. He prayed, "God, enlarge my territory. Let your hand be with me. Keep me from pain" (*see* 1 Chronicles 4:10). He understood that God desired to bring blessing and not defeat. He boldly asked for blessing. Scripture records that God heard and answered his prayer, and that Jabez attained greater happiness and reputation than his brothers.

What is God's desire for his Church? The church I attended as a boy resembled a fortress. With red brick walls, it was a towering "bulwark never failing." When I first read Matthew 16:18—". . . the gates of Hades will not overcome it"—I envisioned the Christians huddled safely within the citadel, while the demons of hell raged outside trying to break down the church doors.

It wasn't until I became a church planter that God gave me a second look at that verse, and did I do a double take! I had assumed that hell was on the offense and the Church on the defense, but according to this verse, the opposite is true. The gates of hell are being broken down, from the outside in, by the Church! It is Satan and his demons who are cowering in their citadel, and the bars aren't holding. The Church is a battering ram in the hands of Christ, and the ramparts of hell are failing rapidly.

God desires to bless his Church. He desires to bless you as a pastor, church planter, or Christian leader. Have you asked him for that blessing? Have you said, "Jesus, I confess that you are the Master Builder of your Church, and that I am merely a subcontractor. But I want to know specifically what part you would have me play"?

The Core of Vision

My father modeled for me how a man should walk with God. One thing that my father often said still stands in my mind above all else:

"My definition of success is very simple. Find out what it is that God wants you to do—and do it."

Time and time again, when I don't know what other steps to take, my life has boiled down to that simple formula. What is it that God wants me to do? Many times I have discovered that the hard part lies not so much in the finding as in the doing.

If God has called you to be a pastor, church planter, or Christian leader, what does God desire for your church? God clearly explains the fundamental vision for all churches in Matthew 28:18–20:

> Then Jesus came to them and said, "All authority in heaven and on earth has been given to me. Therefore go and make disciples of all nations, baptizing them in the name of the Father and of the Son and of the Holy Spirit, and teaching them to obey everything I have commanded you. And surely I will be with you always, to the very end of the age."

We are to make disciples, baptize them, and teach them to obey everything Jesus has commanded us. Traditionally we cite this passage as our impetus for missions work, and that is correct. But the passage itself is far too universal to limit it only to missions. Christ is talking to his disciples; it is his summary command before his ascension. If there were any single piece of instruction, any single command we could point to and say, "This is his command which we must obey," then this is it.

Disciple making is the foundational scriptural vision for churches. Yet it's interesting how few churches truly have disciple making at the core of their vision—if they have a vision at all! By their action, the mission of most churches is more closely related to an exclusive country club than an organization striving to make more and better disciples.

CBC established its purpose by putting disciple making right up front, into its purpose statement:

> Our purpose is to glorify God by making disciples of all people groups and multiplying churches so that believers worship God, win unbelievers to Christ, and become more like Christ.

Components of Vision

Vision has two interdependent components: faith and tenacity. Throughout the Old Testament are examples of how each works to fulfill vision.

God told the children of Israel, under Joshua's leadership, that he was going to bring them across the Jordan and give them the city of

Jericho. God required faith in his promise in order for the Levitical priests who bore the ark of the covenant upon their shoulders to step into the flood-swelled waters of the Jordan, with possibly thousands of residents of Jericho lining the opposite shore. Their faith doubtless was reinforced by the miracle which occurred—the drying up of the waters so that the entire contingent of Israelites could pass.

No doubt they came before the walls of Jericho swelled with faith, and ready to conquer. Why, then, did God ask them to wait seven days and to patiently pass around the city once each day, and seven times on the final day, before he effected the victory? Certainly God was capable of bringing down the walls at the first approach of the Israelites. Why waste all that time marching and waiting? After all, there were other cities to conquer. The Israelites had exercised the preliminary faith in the vision God had given Joshua, but now it was a question of extending their faith through tenacity.

God promised Abraham that he and his wife, Sarah, would have a child in their old age. The New Testament assures us that "Abraham believed God, and it was reckoned to him as righteousness" (*see* Genesis 15:6). Still he had to wait for years and years before seeing God's promise fulfilled. God tested and refined Abraham's faith. If it was sufficiently tenacious, it was true faith.

One night Jacob met a man whom he identified as the angel of the Lord. No doubt the angel of the Lord wanted to bless Jacob, but he acted as if he would pass by without blessing Jacob. Jacob believed in God's blessing, and he stayed and wrestled with the angel of the Lord until morning. And he was wounded in the process! He said, "I will not let you go unless you bless me" (Genesis 32:26). He was tenacious in his desire to experience God's blessing. Jacob pleased God with this tenacious faith, so God gave Jacob the blessing of Israel: "Your descendants will be like the grains of sand on the seashore" (*see* Genesis 22:17).

If you are like most church-growth leaders, you fervently believe that God will give a vision, and you may experience some early blessings. You have no doubt that God heartily desires you to help build a network of growing and reproducing churches. Yet God may play hard to get. He may require that you tenaciously cling to your vision, that you wrestle with him for his blessing. Perhaps the fulfillment of your vision is many years down the road. Like Moses, you may not even live to see it! Yet God is faithful to honor that tenacious, visionizing faith of his elect.

The Role of Prayer

Many people, pastors and church planters among them, live as though they consider prayer a last resort weapon in life's battles. If all else fails, we get down on our knees. We see prayer as a spiritual atom bomb, so to speak. We try things our own way, and when our own way doesn't work, we cry out to God.

The Apostle Paul offers a somewhat different view of prayer:

> For though we live in the world, we do not wage war as the world does. The weapons we fight with are not the weapons of the world. On the contrary, they have divine power to demolish strongholds. We demolish arguments and every pretension that sets itself up against the knowledge of God, and we take captive every thought to make it obedient to Christ.
>   2 Corinthians 10:3–5

The reality is that we are involved in spiritual warfare. Unseen, it rages all around us. Battles are won or lost, and we often attribute these to fate, luck, or coincidence. Yet as you read through Scripture you become more keenly aware that so much of what we attribute to accident is in reality a result of spiritual design. Prayer, as our only true spiritual weapon, is not simply the preparation for the battle: *Prayer is the battle.*

One of my favorite church planters is Tom Nebel, a dynamic young pastor working with Baptist General Conference Churches in Wisconsin. Three years ago, fresh out of Denver Seminary, Tom planted his first church, Community Church of Whitewater, Wisconsin. Recently I had the privilege of attending his church on their third anniversary, the very Sunday their first daughter church began meeting in a neighboring town.

One of the reasons for the success of Tom's church is that he has bathed every step in prayer. Tom believed God would give them twenty people for the first meeting of his infant church, so he prayed faithfully to that end. He set up twenty chairs for the first meeting, but when all the people had filed in, one chair remained empty.

"For a moment I was very discouraged," Tom remembers. "But then, I saw a woman wearing a very large coat." Tom soon learned that the woman was eight months pregnant.

Few would doubt that King David was a man blessed by God. He was Israel's most successful, prosperous, and God-fearing king at that point. Yet David's psalms and prayers reflect that he was a man who lived on the edge, and he lived on that edge in prayer. His life was filled with harrowing pursuits and narrow escapes, with near disasters and would-be calamities. He forever was pleading with God to save his neck. Just as often he was thanking and praising God for intervening in the nick of time. God always gave David just what he truly needed (not just what David thought he needed), at just the right time, because David prayed.

Let's be completely honest here. Church leadership as a vocation will be no less harrowing, and no less dangerous. You doubtless will have many close calls. But you don't have a prayer if you're not willing to spend time on your knees.

Planting or growing churches puts you on the front lines of spiritual warfare. Anyone on the front lines will catch a lot of flak. Your shield of faith will be extinguishing a great many of the enemy's fiery darts, and the sword of the Spirit, which is the Word of God, will find itself handily employed between the chinks of many a foe's armor.

But you'll find the key in Ephesians 6:18: "And pray in the Spirit on all occasions with all kinds of prayers and requests. With this in mind, be alert and always keep on praying for all the saints."

A Prayer Team: Mandatory Equipment

One of the most common but devastating mistakes a church leader can make is to launch upon a ministry venture alone. Too many leaders burn out for lack of a support group of peers—or other pastors, people in ministry, or church planters with whom they can test ideas, seek wisdom, and unload burdens. Men in particular seem to think that their machismo requires them to operate in a vacuum without peer support, and have much to learn from the more highly advanced art of group relationship practiced by many women.

More important than a peer support group, however, is the formation of a group of people gifted in and committed to the art and practice of intercessory prayer on your behalf. This group needn't be large, but it must be faithful.

I recently lost one of my dearest friends, a woman whom I am sure when she arrived at the threshold of heaven, discovered that she had played a much greater role than she had imagined in the attainment of any fruit which has come and will come from my ministry. Her name was Rose Schuster. Early in my pastoral ministry, she committed herself to praying daily for the advancement of God's kingdom through my ministry. Rose, who truly had the spiritual gift of intercession, counted it a privilege and great joy to pray for me. Every day for eight years she kept me, our church, and our daughter churches before the throne of Christ.

Before Rose went home to be with Jesus, she told me: "I may not be able to see any longer, or to do anything with my hands. But I still can pray for you. As long as I am able to do that, I will be happy."

Other equally faithful prayer warriors are on my team of intercessors. But I suspect that if all pastors or church planters had only one Rose Schuster on their team of intercessors, they could revolutionize churches throughout the world overnight.

Vision in the Growing Church

Visionizing faith and prayer is the single most important principle that a Christian leader can employ. In preparation for writing this book, we interviewed dozens of church planters and pastors of growing churches across the country in an attempt to determine what common factors healthy growing churches share. The most universal fact emerging from our research was this: *It is the personal vision of a pastor or church planter, and his or her ability to communicate that vision, that drives churches to growth.*

Wally Hostetter was minister of evangelism at a large, well-established Presbyterian church when the small and struggling Faith Church in Rochester, Michigan, asked him to serve as their pastor. For two years, he declined. He saw that the church was unsure of its identity, experiencing many problems, and headed for failure.

After much prayer, Wally finally accepted the pastorate with one condition: The congregation had to agree wholeheartedly with his vision. Wally's vision was a list of twenty-one items detailing his conception of the ideal church. Although it contained some items as esoteric as "no sacred cows" and some as pragmatic as "the pastor's calling to his family comes before his calling to the church," in reality the list was a statement of Wally's vision for the church.

The few who did not agree with Wally's list concerning the ideal church left the church, and those remaining bound themselves to his vision. In a few short years, a united Faith Church experienced an annual growth rate as high as 45 percent.

Wally doesn't worry about losing people who don't agree with his vision for the church. "We do try to find out precisely why they've left, but the needs of the kingdom are far greater than the needs of single individuals. God has other churches for those people who have a different vision. But he's called us to this vision and ministry."

Michael Brodeur, pastor of Vineyard Christian Fellowship in San Francisco agrees. "The issue central to our success has been our ability to identify who we are and what we want to accomplish. In my first two church-planting projects, which ended in failure, I never felt I could endorse fully what was happening. I invited people to church with a sense of reservation. I didn't own the structure; it didn't reflect my personal values. It was someone else's vision. At Vineyard, too, we have lost momentum every time the church has moved away from my personal vision."

Vision can, and often does, emerge from failure. Tom Nebel also points to his involvement in a "dead, strangling church" as a source of vision. But why not learn from the failures of others instead?

For some pastors, planting their own church is their only option when they can't find an established church that will allow them to fulfill that vision. Dieter Zander says one of the reasons he planted a church was his personality. "I didn't fit into a normal church. I'd always wanted things like contemporary worship and very practical messages. My vision for New Song has flowed from who I am, and how God over the course of time has shaped me."

It sounds simple enough that the leader of an organization—in the case of a church, its senior pastor—should espouse a personal vision which feeds the organization's corporate vision. To do this, though, you will need a carefully arrived at and clearly communicated vision. The following action plan will help you through this step-by-step process.

Action Steps

Spend time in personal prayer. Prayer and worship precede and produce ministry. To have effective, consistent times of prayer, you'll need to select:

A place. Choose a place that will allow you to concentrate your undisturbed attention upon God. If possible, choose someplace you can be alone enough to feel comfortable talking out loud, singing, and even shouting praises.

A plan. Don't enter your prayer time unarmed. Plan how you will use your time for maximum benefit. Have a prayer list and a journal where you can record your impressions. You also might want to have song sheets, a worship tape, or a devotional study guide to get the juices flowing.

A partner. Nothing helps us to develop consistency in prayer as much as someone who will hold us accountable to pray. Having a partner also multiplies exponentially the power of prayer, by Christ's own admonition: ". . . if two of you on earth agree about anything you ask for, it will be done for you by my Father in heaven. For where two or three come together in my name, there am I with them" (Matthew 18:19, 20).

A period. Reserve a specific time slot in your schedule for prayer, and protect it. Generally, following the pattern of Christ, the earlier the better, but make it your choice, most productive time of the day, and thus honor God.

Schedule occasional extended times to meet with God.

Recruit an intercessor team to pray for you daily and with you periodically. Enlist at least three committed people on the team; at least one of them should have the spiritual gift of intercession. *Communicate at least monthly with them.* Use a prayer bulletin which not only keeps your intercessors informed of needs, but also presents praises.

Dream with others who share your vision (Ephesians 3:20, 21).
Identify your network of mentors and others who will support your church-planting project. Meet regularly with them for prayer and planning. Proverbs 15:22 advises us: "Plans fail for lack of counsel, but with many advisers they succeed."

For the past eight years I have scheduled monthly conferences with the pastoral staff at my church. Every month we spend two days together on an overnight prayer, vision, planning, and troubleshooting session. Our most valuable ministry accomplishments have come from these sessions.

Formulate your vision. Ask yourself the following questions:
If I had unlimited resources, what could I believe God for?
What does God want to do with his Church through us?

Trust God for increasingly greater ways to serve him through growth.

Set faith goals and establish a workable plan. Ask God for a vision for your church in each of the nine other principles:
Effective Pastoral Leadership

Culturally Relevant Philosophy of Ministry
   What will your church look like? What is your church's person-
   ality? Its style?
Celebrative and Reflective Worship
   How does your worship style help people respond to the person
   and work of God? Is there an appropriate balance between
   celebration and reflection?
Holistic Disciple Making
   Whom could you reach? What needs can you meet? Determine
   your target group.
Expanding Network of Cell Groups
   How can you best care for people? What will accountability
   relationships look like? Who could lead cell groups?
Developing and Resourcing Leaders
   Who can share the burden of ministry? How will you develop
   and resource people?
Mobilizing Believers According to Spiritual Gifts
   How can you help everyone use their spiritual gifts in ministry?
Appropriate and Productive Programming
   What ministry systems and programs does your church need?
   What will meet the needs of the community?
Starting Churches That Reproduce
   How many new churches can you believe God for?

**Proceed to the remaining principles to find out what God wants you
to do—*then do it!***

Evaluate and make mid-course corrections as you go. Planning is an
ongoing process. Trust God to guide you!

Principle 2

Effective Pastoral Leadership

It was he [Christ] who gave some to be apostles, some to be prophets, some to be evangelists, and some to be pastors and teachers, to prepare God's people for works of service, so that the body of Christ may be built up until we all reach unity in the faith and in the knowledge of the Son of God and become mature, attaining to the whole measure of the fullness of Christ.

Ephesians 4:11–13

What do followers expect of and deserve from leaders? This question is crucial for pastors, whose organizations lie well within the definition of a service industry.

Recently James Kouzes and Barry Posner surveyed more than twenty-six hundred top-level managers from all over the United States to determine precisely what it is that constitutes superior executive leadership. They reported the results in their book, *The Leadership Challenge.*[1]

At the top of the list of what followers expect from leaders is *honesty.* The perception of dishonesty in government may be the single largest complaint that governed peoples lodge against the politicians who govern them. In Kouzes's and Posner's survey, 85 percent of the respondents indicated the first thing followers expect of leaders is that they be persons worthy of their trust.

Followers expect both transparency in communication and honesty in action. A pastor's behavior, on stage and off, is what provides the evidence of honesty in life-style—a consistency between words and deeds.

Saddleback Valley Community Church has grown from zero to four thousand in only eight years. I asked Glen Kreun, executive pastor of the church, what it was about the church's dynamic senior pastor, Dr. Rick Warren, that attracted so many unchurched people.

"Transparency," Glen responded without hesitation. "Because Rick is so transparent, people relate to him. Our church is very casual, no suits and ties, and Rick models this from the pulpit. He uses personal illustrations, opens up his life, and even tells jokes on himself. This disarms even the most disgruntled person, who thinks, 'Maybe I'll listen to what he has to say.' "

In addition, newcomers to Saddleback Valley get to see their pastor in his native environment—at home, through a monthly open house—and they sense that his honesty extends beyond what they see in the pulpit. "It says that I'm human," Rick said. "People see that I live in a normal house with a normal wife and three normal kids. It also keeps me in touch with people, even while our church is growing."

The second trait followers expect of their leaders is *competence*. Sixty-seven percent of the executives surveyed said that a leader must be someone who knows what he or she is doing.

How many pastors truly are competent at the job of being a pastor? Because the pastoral role has been so ill-defined in the past, people don't know how to measure competence in this profession. When a church is attracting new people and growing steadily, its people will point to their pastor's competence as one of the reasons. Effective pastoral leadership always is found in thriving congregations.

Sixty-two percent of the executives surveyed also said that followers expect their leaders to be *forward looking*. A true leader knows where he or she is going, and thus where his or her followers are headed. Followers need that sense of direction, that security, for the future. This is closely related to the vision that you, as a leader, have received from God and are communicating to your church. Have you set a desirable destination for your church? Is it challenging but attainable?

Inspiration is the final crucial expectation that followers have of their leaders. Leaders must have the capacity to enthuse, to excite, and to convey the sense that there's more to life than we yet have experienced—and we'll be there shortly if you hang on for the ride!

Fifty-eight percent of the respondents indicated that inspiration was one of the most important leadership characteristics. Simply having a dream is not enough. Leaders also must have the capacity to communicate it with passion, enthusiasm, energy, and a positive attitude about the future.

What God Expects of Leaders

God's expectations of leaders are more stringent yet. We know that God expects his leaders to be the best servants. After girding himself with a towel, Christ began to observe the Passover supper by washing his disciples' feet—a clear identification with the role of a servant. He then said, "I have set you an example that you should do as I have done for you. I tell you the truth, no servant is greater than his master, nor is a messenger greater than the one who sent him. Now that you know these things, you will be blessed if you do them" (John 13:15–17). Earlier, he had assured them, "The greatest among you will be your servant. For whoever exalts himself will be humbled, and whoever humbles himself will be exalted" (Matthew 23:11, 12). In addition, Ephesians 4:11–13 reveals that God has further expectations of those who lead his flock.

True leaders are called by God. Leadership is given by Christ himself, who designates different kinds of leaders with different assignments, according to his purpose. Some are apostles, some prophets, some evangelists, some pastors, and some teachers.

God has chosen not to endow any one of us with all the gifts and abilities necessary for the body's healthy functioning. How often do we think, "If only everyone in this church had my heart, my zeal, or my abilities"? In reality, if everyone else were just like me, it truly would be a disaster![2] (*See* 2 Corinthians 12:14–27.)

The Purpose of Leadership

No other Scripture passage so clearly states the foundational purpose of pastoral leadership as Ephesians 4:12, 13: "to prepare God's people for works of service, so that the body of Christ may be built up until we all reach unity in the faith and in the knowledge of the Son of God and become mature, attaining to the whole measure of the fullness of Christ."

Pastors often grumble that their churches aren't getting anywhere because the people are so immature. Though the intent is to pass the buck, in reality, this statement is a self-indictment. It is the pastor's job as a leader to cultivate spiritual maturity—in short, godly character expressed via the selfless love, joy, peace, patience, kindness, goodness, faithfulness, gentleness, and self-control which so marked the life of Jesus. *Effective pastors work to develop godly character in the lives of those they lead.*

The main verb Paul used to describe the Christian leader's job in Ephesians 4:12, *to prepare*, is the same Greek word sometimes translated *to equip*, which literally means "to put in working order" or "to repair." It is used in the classical Greek in reference to setting a broken bone and, in the Gospels, to mend a torn net.

The ideal state of a net is to be strong enough to catch and hold fish. A torn net is worthless because a fisherman cannot use it for its intended purpose. If he can repair it, though, the fisherman once again may use it to fulfill that purpose.

God created us to minister, to bring glory to God by serving one another in love. However, we have been torn by sin. In this state of disrepair, we cannot fulfill that purpose effectively. Generally speaking, this is the state in which you can expect to find your congregation. Your job will be to repair those nets so they once again can hold fish.

This is easy to say, but harder to do. Effective leadership does not come easily to anyone, but it can be learned.

Coaching

As a sports fan, I realize how much similarity exists between the job of a pastor and that of a coach. Just as a coach equips his or her team to win, so an effective pastor functions like a coach to cultivate a thriving congregation.

Effective coaches share six common characteristics.

They Establish Challenging But Attainable Goals

The ability to set challenging but attainable goals is the natural outflowing of a leader with a vision for where his or her church is going. As such a person, you may not know precisely how to get there—what the road looks like—but you are well acquainted with your destination.

Since those early days when God gave me a vision for churches, I never have had a problem understanding the goal. At times we have had a challenging but rewarding job of coming to understand the procedure necessary to achieve the goal. But if God has given you a vision for what he desires you accomplish, you'll find the goals themselves generally will be clear.

Setting those goals involves not only having them in your head, but also communicating them in such a way that others will see them as their own. It is easy to say, "In ten years everyone in the state will be a member of our church." You truly may believe it, and it may be true. But as a goal to set before your people, it is challenging, but not attainable.

On the other hand, you may set a goal to raise $200,000 to build a repair garage for your church bus fleet in the next ten years. If your church's income is $50,000 a week, this goal no doubt is achievable. But is it challenging?

The process of goal setting involves taking the larger goals that God has placed before you in your vision—whom he wants you to become, whom you will reach, what kind of body you will be, the daughter churches you will plant—and breaking them into bite-sized morsels or steps along the pathway to fulfillment. They must be specific and measurable. You will work the process from the ultimate goal backward to your current position in order to determine the next step to take to reach your goal.

Don't think that goal setting involves no cost. Goal setting is an important part of your job, and it requires planning, time, and effort. Open your calendar now and schedule goal-setting sessions. Use the following standard until you know how much time you'll need to spend in goal-setting activities:

Weekly	one hour	
Monthly	four hours	(in addition to weekly)
Quarterly	eight hours	(in addition to monthly)

For some of us, setting goals is easy, but ranking those goals so that we focus time and energy on those which are most important is much more difficult. Effective coaches set priorities and stick to them. They put first things first in order to accomplish their goals.

Winning Coaches Recruit Athletes for the Team

The second characteristic of an effective coach is a result of the necessary realization that he alone is not the entire team. Most coaches contribute less when it comes to the physical requirements for winning a game—shooting the baskets, scoring the goals, or even grinding some offending hockey opponent's face into the ice—than even the least of their team members. But the coach does play a key role in determining the outcome of those games by recruiting team players with the potential to win.

C. Peter Wagner, in his outstanding book, *Leading Your Church to Growth*, includes a chapter with the memorable title "Why Bill Bright is Not Your Pastor."[3] Using terms coined by Ralph D. Winter, director of the U.S. Center for World Mission in Pasadena, California, it discusses two ways God wires leaders. Some leaders possess a passion and working style which best lends itself to leadership of *modalities* or people-oriented structures; other leaders have a passion and working style which best lends itself to *sodalities* or task-oriented structures. Local churches generally are led by modality leaders; sodality leaders are so impatient to get the job done (winning the world for Christ, planting churches, feeding the hungry, whatever their passion may be) that they often find themselves sifting out of churches and into missions or specialized ministries. I speak from experience, having left the church I founded, because I felt a specific call of God to serve as a missions executive and work within a framework where I could more effectively resource leaders to plant new churches.

Wagner interestingly observes that growing churches generally are led by sodalic pastors who often have the gifts of leadership and faith. These are the task-oriented men and women who challenge their flocks to stretch beyond themselves, to minister, and to give of themselves in multiplying churches, all those irritant practices which, like the grain of sand in the oyster, defy comfort zones and cause people to respond to God and cause churches to grow. On the other hand are the modalic pastors, who often have gifts of mercy or exhortation, and who personally nurture and care for members in their flocks.

How does all this relate to recruiting athletes? Just this: Sodalic pastors are equipping pastors, focusing on people with potential, and bypassing those who require greater input with less promise of output. They walk around the wounded. Says Michael Brodeur, the sodalic-minded pastor of Vineyard Christian Fellowship in San Francisco: "Spiritual warfare is too intense for us to play around." In contrast, modalic pastors are shepherding pastors who focus on those who are hurting, and are unable to pass up the temptation to spend inordinate amounts of time with TLC sponges.

It's not an issue of caring or not caring for wounded and hurting sheep. It's more like the difference between effective shepherds and ranchers. Although both care deeply for their sheep, they differ dramatically in how they deliver that care. A shepherd administers care to each sheep in a limited flock, but a rancher takes steps to ensure someone else provides personal care to every sheep on the ranch.

A shepherding pastor often discourages others in the church from using their God-given caring gifts because he or she *must* be the chief dispenser of care. Shepherding pastors don't want their churches to grow too large in fear that their work load will exceed their capacity to care individually for each member.

An equipping pastor, on the other hand, focuses time and energy on identifying and releasing the gifts in the body so that all the needs are met. Church growth is not a threat because the ministry, as designed by God, releases all the members of the congregation to serve so that the body ". . . grows and builds itself up in love, as each part does its work" (Ephesians 4:16).

Our Lord Jesus Christ is our model of equipping ministry. He didn't select as his disciples men whom the religious establishment might have considered cream of the crop; instead he chose those diamonds in the rough in whom he saw great hidden potential. It's interesting to note that there was one sophisticate among the ranks of the disciples—one man savvy enough to hobnob with religious leaders and be trusted with the group treasury—Judas Iscariot.

However, it is also interesting that the remainder of the disciples were men selected by Christ after much prayer, no doubt because he discerned they had great spiritual potential. Christ did not simply recruit any hurting soul who happened along his path. He ministered to the ten lepers, but then sent them away to see the priest; he cleansed and healed the demoniac of the Gadarenes, then instructed him to stay among his own people. However, he continued down the road with the disciples whom he had selected to be the future leaders of his movement. These were the men into whom he poured his time and energy.

Selecting leaders, then, is primarily a functional spiritual discernment. Look for humility, willingness to change, and responsiveness to spiritual authority. If you are selecting an individual to fulfill a specific role, examine carefully the candidates' strengths and weaknesses. What are their untapped potentials? What are they willing to believe that God could do in their lives? Spend much time praying about each individual, and then select carefully. Select only a few; then pour your time and energy into developing them.

An effective coach takes two more steps in the recruiting process. While a person is being recruited, the effective coach employs all his or her persuasive skill to sell the newcomer on the benefits of the position or program for which this person was recruited. Then the coach spends the necessary time to orient fully the new player to the fundamentals of the game, the basic knowledge required to get started. The new player needs to understand the place of value that he or she holds in the scheme of things.

Wouldn't it be wonderful to have a church with a reputation for raising up well-equipped leaders? Briarwood Presbyterian Church in Birmingham, Alabama, has equipped leaders so well that they've begun their own seminary/night school to augment the task. Pastor Frank Barker can cite a long list of people equipped through the seminary to serve in positions in the church, or to begin their own churches or serve in missions. He summarizes his philosophy of equipping by looking at the Gospels. "Pour your life into a group of men, just as Jesus did," he advises pastors.

You'll find no shortcut to achieve both of these steps. At this level, you can't delegate this task of discipling your team players. You must put in the hours, both in prayer and in contact.

Inspire the Team to Maximum Performance

Effective pastors find themselves living out their vision. They accomplish leadership by personal example.

Two important tests of your commitment to your vision are your calendar and your checkbook. How you allocate the resources God has given you says more about your faith in the vision than what you say.

Time is one resource that everyone receives in equal amounts. How you manage this resource may spell the difference between success and failure in accomplishing your goals. Ben Franklin said, "Time is the stuff which life is made of. To waste your time is to waste your life. To master time is to control your life." If you truly believe that God has placed his vision before you, and you believe in his ability to accomplish it, you will not hesitate to invest wisely the time required on your part to make your vision a reality.

Money is another test of your commitment to the vision. Your checkbook stands as a testament to what you believe truly is important in life. Pastors must be model servants and stewards in every respect.

The way you fill key leadership positions also has an effect on whether you can inspire your team players to maximum performance. Whether you like it or not, your promotion of a person will be an acknowledgment or affirmation of that person's past ministry performance. If you promote on any other basis—friendship, seniority, knowledge, personal power—you send the entire team a message that achieving your goals is not what it's all about. Affirm people's inherent worth, but the effective, result-oriented pastor promotes only on the basis of achievement (in addition to bibical criteria, of course).

My examination of growing churches across the United States revealed that one of the key aspects of their senior pastors' success as coaches is their ability to share with their players the vision God has given them.

Players like to win, and they want to win. Yet do they truly believe that they *will* win? They look at themselves and are full of doubts. They look at their team and its shortcomings and are full of doubts. Then they look at their coach to see if he, too, is full of doubts. A coach who is full of doubts confirms their worst fears: *We can't win*. But a coach who believes with all his heart that his team *can* win is a coach who inspires his team to winning performance.

One of the main ways to do this is to help people visualize a winning future. Many leaders don't realize this, but herein lies the essence of faith: your ability to create a convincing image of the reality of a future that God plans for you if you only will believe. What does that future look like for your church? If, like Rick Warren, you keep that winning image ever before your players, communicating it at every opportunity, they will begin to catch the vision. As goes the faith of the leader, so goes the faith of the followers.

The Bible contains many examples of this. One that I thoroughly enjoy is the story of Nehemiah. Nehemiah was born at a time when the Hebrew nation was in desperate straits. In bondage to a powerful Babylonian regime, they were for the most part exiled far from their homeland. The Hebrew nation, grown soft and fat because of God's blessing, had forsaken him one time too many, and God exiled them because of their sin. They were scattered, forsaken, and desperate for hope.

The once-glorious city which symbolized the nation's calling, Jerusalem, reflected this hopelessness as well. Its walls were broken down and its buildings in a state of sad disrepair. Desert animals inhabited it and travelers despised it.

God gave to a godly man, Nehemiah, a vision of a Jerusalem redeemed and rebuilt. In obedience, Nehemiah followed God, risking his excellent position in the king's court to take what must have seemed to many a futile journey to Jerusalem to survey the damage and to begin a rebuilding program. He marshaled together a ragtag band of Israelites to whom stories of Jerusalem's greatness must have been only a legend or a dim memory.

The walls were rebuilt, in spite of much opposition and persecution. Those with whom Nehemiah shared his vision turned unreservedly back to express their faith in God, and God poured his blessing upon them in an unprecedented fashion. Then the multitudes of God's chosen responded to him with great rejoicing and brokenness of spirit in a way that much pleased the Lord (*see* Nehemiah 8). And it all started with the vision and courageous obedience of one man.

The best way to inspire people to maximum performance is through storytelling. In his best-selling book, *Thriving on Chaos*, Tom Peters writes: "The best leaders, especially in chaotic conditions (effective generals, leaders of revolutions), almost without exception and at every level, are master users of stories and symbols."[4] Effective leaders employ the tools of allegory and anecdote to stimulate and inspire their followers. We all are familiar with the way Christ himself spoke in parables to accomplish a large portion of his teaching. Jesus knew the human mind well enough to understand the potential of a well-told story to slide past defense mechanisms and to work an internal change in the listener.

Some of the best leaders and preachers are avid clippers. They borrow almost any story that they hear anywhere (not hesitating, of course, to attribute the story's source) and file it until it comes in handy. They read newspapers, magazines, and books (both secular and religious), listen to talk shows, pursuing information that might yield a valuable story. They also have ears planted everywhere; that is, they have friends and co-workers on alert for stories that might prove useful. They always observe life by asking, "How could I use this as an illustration to teach a godly principle or share a vision?"

The advent of the computer age has increased exponentially the capacity to accumulate and access stories on any given subject within seconds. Simple-to-use free-form database management software packages are on the market for less than fifty dollars. They will allow you to type a story, complete with source attribution and a list of key words or a summary, and then store this story and be able to access it at any time simply by commanding the computer to find any key word, phrase, or source name that appears anywhere in the story.

Although going computerized has many dangers (including the hazard of spending too much money or too much time figuring out how the system works or tinkering with it), computers have many outstanding benefits. Used properly, a desktop, portable, or lap-top computer system can be a marvelous tool for increasing a pastor's effectiveness. I wholeheartedly recommend using an outline processor, such as MaxThink,[5] to help sharpen your thinking and communication skills.

Design Strategy

Once goals are set and communicated, a coach presses on to the next task of designing an effective strategy or game plan. Four maxims guide this process.

MAXIMIZE STRENGTHS. So often we focus on weakness. We spend our time trying to figure out where our dikes are leaking, and scramble to make repairs. We could circumvent much of this effort by focusing on areas of strength instead.

This is one of the values of gaining an awareness of the distribution of spiritual gifts throughout your church. Later we will discuss how this can be done. I have learned that the Holy Spirit distributes gifts in different ways among different bodies (or perhaps churches attract certain types of people because of the prevalence of certain gifts). Sometimes, too, gift distribution is linked to the current needs of your church or what particular crossroads you have reached in the life of your church.

Some time ago we realized that we needed to provide advanced, ongoing training in areas of people's spiritual giftedness as a part of the equipping process for which we were responsible. I discovered that the two most predominant gifts of recent incoming members were administration and intercession. As we reflected on this fact, it became clear that the Holy Spirit was speaking to us about the needs of the church through the gift mix of the new members joining the church.

At that time, we were operating a congregation of almost twelve hundred in a single auditorium seating three hundred, and with limited classroom space. Our church was relatively new and our congregation quite young, so our financial base still was tenuous. Our great need was for quality programming administered efficiently and creatively. Staff members of churches with far greater facilities but smaller congregations often have visited our church and expressed shock that we could accomplish so much with such scanty resources.

The crucial developing need of our church was—and now is—quality intercession to solve some critical problems. A very large percentage of our congregation is previously unchurched, and members of our body have many serious personal needs. In addition, we were at a critical juncture at which our limited facility was constricting our growth potential and demand. We desperately needed some God-given insight about how we could address these issues and allow our growth to continue unabated. The predominance of the intercession gift meant we could bathe all our problems in quality intercessory prayer, and so as the church surges ahead, we now are removing obstacles which otherwise could affect negatively CBC's momentum.

We offered our first two advanced training seminars on the gifts of administration and intercession, addressing crucial congregational needs and building on the strengths of the new members as well as the established ones.

EXPLOIT OPPORTUNITIES. An effective strategy for team productivity recognizes the opportunities at hand and seeks to use these for maximum benefit. We realized early in the life of our church that our target audience was a commuting population. Rancho Cucamonga is a suburb of the busy twin metropolitan centers of Los Angeles and Orange County, and a large number of our people spend two to three hours or more each working day on the freeways commuting to and from work. Because most have audiotape players in their automobiles, this presented a great opportunity for us to accomplish some of our training goals. Rather than inundate our people with written materials, our strategy has been to produce audio teaching tapes at every opportunity. This has proven an effective strategy because so many people have the opportunity for concentrated listening time while stalled in traffic on the freeways.

Conduct Team Practices

DEVELOP THE SKILLS OF INDIVIDUALS, AS WELL AS THOSE OF SUBUNITS WORKING TOGETHER. Can you imagine a Broadway play without rehearsals? It would be a guaranteed disaster, no matter how good the actors. Likewise, even the most gifted leadership team courts disaster if it fails to rehearse sufficiently its plan of attack.

Rehearsals have three primary benefits. First, they help the players to visualize success. What is the goal of the activities we are planning? What will our church look like if we succeed? This step is simply another opportunity for the coach to instill his vision in his followers.

Second, rehearsals allow the players to practice, without substantial risk of failure, the skills necessary for the team to win the game. Players in an evangelism-training rehearsal, for instance, would practice developing skills such as identifying their networks of relationships, developing a plan for friendship evangelism, writing, polishing, and orally rehearsing their testimonies, and considering the range of methods for assimilating their friends and relatives into the church's life.

And third, rehearsals generate confidence in the players. Confidence is a necessary component for winning games. How many times have you seen an aggressive team perform very well in the first three quarters only to have a negative experience which caused them to lose confidence in the fourth quarter? As they waver before their opponents and their opponents gain confidence, the game can reverse itself

completely in an astonishingly short time. This has less to do with the
teams' respective skills than with their confidence level or lack thereof.

AFFIRM TEAM PLAYERS CONSISTENTLY AND CORRECT WHEN NECESSARY.   One of
the most common sins of omission to afflict leaders is their failure to
affirm their team players. Coaches use different styles in relating to
their teams. Some wield a big stick and are greatly feared by their team;
others are fatherly figures who never fail to spew words of kindness
even in the face of utter defeat. But in reality, a hybrid of the two
temperaments is the breed which wins the game for the effective coach.

Just as Scripture commands us both to love and fear God—just as we
can trust in his absolute care for us, as well as the absolute surety of his
chastisement should we stray—so players on winning teams both love
and fear their coaches. Their coaches consistently affirm positive behavior and correct negative behavior. I never have hesitated to correct
anyone under my care whose actions or lack thereof work contrary to
our values and goals. This includes even small corrections such as
instructing a person to park his car at the furthest end of the parking
lot to leave room up front for visitors. Likewise, I always try to notice
and commend such positive behavior. Your team players should feel
that you take absolutely nothing for granted.

Winning Coaches Cultivate Team Spirit in a Winning Environment

This cultivation process encompasses five steps. First, value each
member's unique contribution to the group. Realize that every player
on your team can do *something* better than anyone else. Your job as
coach is to help each one discover what that thing is, and then do
it—not so to puff anyone up, but so everyone can realize they have
places as valuable and needed members of the team.

Second, applaud individual accomplishment as team accomplishment. Although you will recognize and affirm each individual's value
to the organization, the contribution one makes belongs to the organization as a whole and you must celebrate it as such. This will require
much biblical humility on your part, and will allow you to model this
practice before your team members. Allow others to share team accomplishments regardless of whose individual efforts they result from.
The accomplishment of a fine athlete setting a record, regardless of the
sport, would be impossible if it were not for the various parts of his
body working in unison, each giving its utmost.

Third, build group cohesiveness. Your assignment is to help all members see how they fit into the larger group, and how they need the other members of the group in order to be effective.

Primarily, group cohesiveness occurs only when the fourth step carefully is observed. A winning team spends time together as a group, experiencing both difficult and rewarding times. Be sure to schedule fun and relaxing activities. Some of the most creative ideas and best work of our ministry team at CBC resulted from times when we all sat and soaked in a Jacuzzi, simply enjoying being together and interacting with one another. You never can eat enough meals together. Likewise, group games and exercise can be a very healthy practice for your leadership team. Whatever the activity, be sure to schedule regular, extended periods of time for your team to retreat and spend time together.

The fifth step is to plan regular celebrations. Make it a top priority to embark on no project or set no goal without first planning how you will celebrate the successful completion of that project or goal. Failing to celebrate your wins together will erode, perhaps irreparably, your team's enthusiasm for embracing future, more challenging goals the Lord sets before you.

What God Expects of Followers

We have spoken at length about the pastoral leader's responsibilities before God. But what are the responsibilities of followers? It has been said, "Good followers make good leaders." This is true because everyone is a follower of someone. The new senior pastor of CBC, Dr. Rob Acker, who served for eight years as my associate pastor, says that his six-year-old daughter asked him why she needed to obey her mother. "Because Mommy is your boss," he explained.

"Daddy," she said, "I know who your boss is."

"Who, sweetheart?"

"God is your boss. And the people at church. And Mommy."

Rob says she ran off quickly, not wanting to give him opportunity to correct her on the latter count.

Moses, one of the greatest leaders in the Bible, represented in almost all points what it means to exercise godly leadership. However, in most respects, the people whom God gave Moses to lead were so inept as followers that Yahweh barely was restrained on several occasions from wiping them out completely and starting over again. As it was, the entire generation had to spend forty years wandering the desert and all but two in that generation would die there before the nation sufficiently was cleansed and was able to follow Joshua to victory in the Promised Land.

Followership is a serious problem in our particular culture, partly as a result of our democratic heritage and the me-first attitude which unfortunately has developed as an abuse of this heritage. Generally speaking, we make lousy sheep. Many churches go through pastors as a hypochondriac goes through doctors. We have bought into the politics of our governing bodies and developed a bad habit of church leadership by consensus. Very rare is the church which does not have a constitution defining the voting privileges of its congregation and the limits of authority of its pastors.

In his book *Leading Your Church to Growth*, C. Peter Wagner exposes the dangers of leadership by consensus and devotes an entire chapter to discussing the positive correlation between healthy, growing churches and those which are highly responsive to the strong leadership of their pastors. In two columns, Wagner lays out the biblically mandated roles of leaders and those of followers, then says: "It takes less than thirty seconds to look up and down those two columns and to be deeply impressed with the seriousness of biblical leadership and followership."[6]

Hebrews 13:17 instructs followers:

Obey your leaders and submit to their authority. They keep watch over you as men who must give an account. Obey them so that their work will be a joy, not a burden, for that would be of no advantage to you.

Earlier in this chapter I noted that leadership was granted only by divine appointment. But being a senior pastor with a flock responsive enough to make me grateful to be their leader, I also realized that *leadership is a gift given by those who follow*. If you have the means to enforce involuntary followership, you can be a lord; but you never can be a leader unless God blesses you with those who will follow you willingly.

However, this acknowledgment does not absolve the responsibility of those who have submitted themselves to the authority of spiritual leadership to follow those leaders. The language of Scripture is strong: "Obey your leaders and submit to their authority." In this culture we don't like words such as *obey* and *submit*. As you teach your people these concepts no doubt you must be sensitive to cultural contexts. But at times you will need to lay it on the line with your church members: "Lead, follow, or get out of the way!"

As a senior pastor, each year in early January I spent extended time seeking to hear what the Lord was saying to this body over which he had given me responsibility. I then presented what came to be known as the state-of-the-church address to communicate whatever I had heard to my congregation.

In January 1988 the message the Lord gave me was extraordinarily clear—and extraordinarily uncomfortable. But I determined to tell it precisely as the Lord said it was.

At the time, we were what is known in church-growth terms as sociologically strangulated. That is, we packed out each of our five worship services (five being the maximum number that our leadership team could handle without sure consignment to an insane asylum) with well over 80 percent of the available seating space filled. Worse yet, our Sunday-school classrooms were jammed tighter than sardine tins, and our parking lot was filled to capacity. When newcomers came, as they did in droves, for all practical purposes we were turning them away to go somewhere else. This broke my heart.

As I looked out over the five congregations that weekend I became painfully aware of another phenomenon peculiar to our body. Although many Baptist churches have membership levels much higher than attendance, in our church—as in a number of other growing churches we surveyed—the opposite was true. Membership is a tangible step of faith for committed believers to fulfill our requirements for body life—salvation and baptism, regular attendance, ministry using one's spiritual gift, involvement in cell-group life, and financial support. Our congregations therefore were filled with people who enjoyed coming and having their hearts uplifted by positive, dynamic worship, but who were uncommitted to the rigors of membership. Our attendance was more than twice our membership level.

The essence of my state-of-the-church address that January was: "If you've been sitting in these chairs for a year or more soaking up all this blessing of God like a sponge, but are unwilling to wring it out by identifying yourself with this body and committing to membership, then there may be another church home for you elsewhere." I could see shock rolling over the audience in waves. A few people did leave, but their seats quickly were filled by newcomers; and many more were challenged to commit themselves to identify with our church. The rate of new membership shot up during 1988 to *double* that of 1987. Once in a while, we need to challenge people to confront the reality of God's desire that they yield themselves more fully to the spiritual authority vested by him in their leaders.

We find another significant biblical responsibility of followers in
1 Thessalonians 5:12, 13:

> Now we ask you, brothers, to respect those who work hard among you,
> who are over you in the Lord and who admonish you. Hold them in the
> highest regard in love because of their work. Live in peace with each other.

Scripture consistently urges respect for authority, whether that be
governmental authority, family authority, or church authority. Such
respect is due, not simply because God has placed pastors in authority,
but also because of their work. God will judge those churches which
mistreat and abuse their hard-working pastors.

As I have ministered I have taken great pains, for my own sake, to
be always in accountability relationships. That means I not only have
submitted myself to God, but also I have been careful to be accountable
to mentors or to a board of directors. Such submission to spiritual
authority is the check and balance that prevents fiascos and scandals
that make newspaper headlines. Everyone needs someone to whom he
can be spiritually accountable, someone who has the fortitude to pull
on the reins when he begins to wander out of line, as we all do at some
point.

Do you have someone to whom you are accountable? A mentor? A
denominational board? A church board? Submit yourself to that spiritual authority as unto God. Be a good follower, and you will be a good
leader.

Evaluate Your Potential

Effective pastors carefully have studied and have arrived at an accurate view of their own strengths and weaknesses. Then they exercise
the humility and the ability to surround themselves with people who
complement them.

If you never have launched on a serious effort to "know thyself,"
now is the time to start! Many tools are available to help you cultivate
effectiveness as a pastoral leader. I'll name just a few here.

The Personal Profile System by Performax, more commonly known
as the DISC Test, is an assessment instrument found so valuable by our
church staff that we administered it to all our staff and ministry leaders.
Jim Dethmer, founding pastor of Grace Fellowship Church in Baltimore, uses the Personal Profile System for every new member. Although the DISC Test primarily deals with your working style, it also
has applications for other areas of your life, such as the way you interact
with your spouse.

The DISC Test uses a word-association/self-description instrument to establish a statistically significant profile of your working style as you feel others perceive it, as you perceive it, and how it shifts under pressure. Your score creates a pattern—such as achiever, specialist, objective thinker, or appraiser—which more specifically describes your working style, often-experienced emotions, goals, standard of judgment of others, strategy for influencing others, value to the organization, overuses, tendencies under pressure, fears, and the type of tolerances you need to be more effective, as well as the type of people you need around yourself. The overwhelming majority of people to whom we have administered the DISC Test have found it to be accurate and very helpful in understanding their behavior and working with others.[7]

Bobb Biehl, president of Masterplanning Group International, has developed a useful analysis instrument called the Role Preference Inventory. This tool helps you analyze yourself or your co-workers to discover the roles with which you are most comfortable. For example, it will help you determine whether you function best as a captain or as a strong player. The test helps you to analyze further your preferred role by determining whether you are a designer, a designer/developer, a developer, a developer/manager, or a manager.[8]

The Meyers-Briggs instrument is another valuable tool for analyzing how a person receives and processes information from the world around him. Meyers-Briggs uses four sets of polarities when analyzing respondents: introvert vs. extrovert, sensing vs. intuition, thinking vs. feeling, judging vs. perceiving. Meyers-Briggs uses combinations of these four polarities to arrive at general descriptions of the person taking the test.[9]

If you are serious about discovering more about your own strengths or weaknesses and what bearing they will have on the task of planting or pastoring a church, you also might want to consider a customized assessment. Dr. Thomas Graham, director of the Center for Organizational and Ministry Development, conducts assessment centers for denominational and missions organizations to evaluate potential church planting, pastoral, or missionary candidates.[10] Dr. Charles Ridley, a licensed psychologist who teaches at Fuller Theological Seminary, specializes in church-planter selection. He can arrange a personal evaluation which involves a day-long battery of tests and interviews.[11] A price tag is attached to such an analysis, but the long-term results are well worth it.

Action Steps

Cultivate your personal integrity.

Study 1 Timothy 3:1–13. How do you need to grow in each of the following areas?

Is your heart set on being an overseer? What is your view of the nobility of such an assignment? Are you above reproach in . . .

Your relationship with your spouse?

> Temperance?
> Self-control?
> Respectability?
> Hospitality?
> Ability to teach?

Are you . . .

> Sober minded?
> Gentle?
> Not quarrelsome?
> Not a lover of money?

Do you manage your family well and see that your children obey you with proper respect?

Are you seasoned (proven, tested) in the faith?

Do you have a good reputation among the unchurched?

Are you . . .

> Worthy of respect? Sincere?
> An exerciser of moderation?
> Honest in business dealings?

Can you hold on to the deep truths of the faith with a clear conscience? In other words, do you believe what you teach?

Is your spouse worthy of respect, not a malicious talker but temperate and trustworthy in everything?

Set measurable personal-growth goals in the above areas of character development.

Establish a proactive approach to ministry.

Review your appointments for the past three months. What do they tell about what truly is important to you? How are you spending your time? What changes do you need to make?

Prayerfully establish your personal priorities for ministry.

Set a calendar of appointments that reflects your priorities for ministry.

Growth Checklist

Growth Area	Able to Train Others	Very Effective	Adequate	Needs Help
Honesty/transparency				
Competence				
Skilled leader				
Forward looking				
Receives vision				
Communicates vision				
Inspiring				
Enthuses, motivates				
Divine mandate for leadership				
Self-knowledge				
Strengths				
Growth areas				
Goal setter				
Challenging				
Achievable				
Prioritized				
Team recruiter				
Spends time in prayer				
Sees potential in others				
Sells program to newcomers				
Orients newcomers				
Team Inspirer				
Models stewardship				
Promotes by performance				
Shares the vision				
Instills confidence				
Expert storyteller				
Increases productivity				
Exploits opportunities				
Maximizes strengths				
Rehearses the game plan				
Affirms and corrects				
Cultivates team spirit				
Values each member				
Applauds team accomplishments				
Builds group cohesiveness				
Spends time with team				
Plans regular celebrations				
Is a good follower				
Obeys and submits to authority				
Respects authority				

Sharpen your coaching skills.
Review the following chart and evaluate where you're strong and where you need to grow.

Read and discuss C. Peter Wagner's *Leading Your Church to Growth* (*Ventura, Calif.: Regal Books, 1984*).

Read and discuss James M. Kouzes and Barry Z. Pasner's *The Leadership Challenge* (San Francisco; Jossey-Bass, 1987).

Notes

1. *See* James M. Kouzes and Barry Z. Posner, *The Leadership Challenge* (San Francisco: Jossey-Bass, 1987), 15–27, for an expanded discussion of their study.

2. For an elaboration of this concept, see the book I coauthored with Carl George, *Leading and Managing Your Church* (Old Tappan, N.J.: Fleming H. Revell Company, 1987).

3. C. Peter Wagner, *Leading Your Church to Growth* (Ventura, Calif.: Regal Books, 1984), pp. 141-165.

4. Tom Peters, *Thriving on Chaos* (New York: Alfred A. Knopf, 1987), p. 418.

5. Available by writing Neil Larson, MaxThink Software, 230 Crocker Ave., Piedmont, CA 94610, or calling (415) 428-0104.

6. Wagner, *Leading Your Church to Growth*, p. 110.

7. Order the *Personal Profile System* from the Charles E. Fuller Institute for Evangelism and Church Growth, P.O. Box 91990, Pasadena, CA 91109-1990.

8. The *Role Preference Inventory* is available from the Masterplanning Group International, Box 6128, Laguna Niguel, CA 92677.

9. You can receive an introduction to the Meyers-Briggs Inventory by reading *Please Understand Me* by David Keirsey and Marilyn Bates (Del Mar, Calif.: Prometheus Nemesis Book Co., 1978).

10. Contact Dr. Graham's office at P.O. Box 904, La Habra, CA 90603-0904.

11. Write Dr. Ridley at 180 N. Oakland, Pasadena, CA 91182.

Principle 3

Culturally Relevant Philosophy of Ministry

Though I am free and belong to no man, I make myself a slave to everyone, to win as many as possible. To the Jews I became like a Jew, to win the Jews. To those under the law I became like one under the law (though I myself am not under the law), so as to win those under the law. To those not having the law I became like one not having the law (though I am not free from God's law but am under Christ's law), so as to win those not having the law. To the weak I became weak, to win the weak. I have become all things to all men so that by all possible means I might save some. I do all this for the sake of the gospel, that I may share in its blessings.

1 Corinthians 9:19–23

When I first began the task of planting a church in Rancho Cucamonga, I went door to door and talked to the people of the community. I informally interviewed hundreds of unchurched people. My goal was to understand the attitudes, values, and needs of the people in my community.

As a basis for the interview I used the following Community Survey Questions:

1. Are you an active member of a nearby church?
2. What do you think is the greatest need in this community?
3. Why do you think most people don't attend church?
4. If you were looking for a church in the area, what kinds of things would you look for?
5. What advice would you give me as the pastor of a new church?
6. Are you interested in getting more information about this new church?[1]

As a result of my survey I discovered that generally people had been turned off not by the message of Christ himself, but by the way Christ had been presented. The major stumbling blocks included hymnals and pipe organ music, sixteenth-century English, and pressure to attend, give financially, or join the church. However, people were very receptive to spiritual things and the genuine message of the Gospel.

Wally Hostetter, senior pastor of Faith Evangelical Presbyterian Church, had a similar idea. Their first summer in Detroit, Wally wanted to find out how he could attract people from the surrounding community to his fledgling church. He hired an advertising agency which designed an eye-catching, postcard-sized survey that began: "Your opinion is important. Why do you think most people don't go to church?"

The 2 percent response, impressive for a mail survey, yielded a gold mine of good advice. The number one response was that all the church wants is your money; second, sermons are boring and don't relate to my life; third, people in churches are "holier than thou"; and fourth, church has nothing to offer my children.

Wally used this advice to plan not only his church, but also how he would present his church to the public through advertising. With ads like "Don't bring your wallet," "We're not holier than thou," and "We won't make you yawn," he sought to assure the community that this new church had broken the mold of their perception of a church.

He believes that the local church's mission is to fill itself with people willing to "break all the traditions, and do away with all the junk that's in the way of reaching lost people for Christ. The great hindrance to reaching the unchurched is the Church." When Wally came to the newly established church as founding pastor, he let everyone know he felt very strongly about one thing: "We will have no sacred cows," he said, "and if we see one coming over the hill, we'll shoot it!

"The only thing that should offend a person coming into your church should be the message of Christ crucified," Wally says. "And even then, present it as the message of hope that it is, so that people may leave feeling better and more hopeful than when they came in. This isn't positive thinking. It's the Good News."

An amazing phenomenon in the twentieth-century church is that we still are stuck in forms of worship and ministry which are more culturally appropriate to the nineteenth century. The robes, the pipe organ, the hymnals, the order of worship, and the nature and place of the sermon all are vestiges of nineteenth-century culture. They still may be appropriate culturally, to some extent, primarily in those churches targeting older people or those who have some religious heritage. However, because people under the age of thirty, with no church background, comprise the largest percentage of the population, what we should be seeing is a majority of churches manifesting more contemporary cultural forms of worship and ministry.

Many sociologists describe a clear line of demarcation in this country between pre-war and post-war believers. Even though the vast majority of Christians are post-war believers, having received Christ in the 1950s or later, the power base in many churches still resides with the pre-war believers. This effectively narrows the choice of churches where believers may be involved with forms of worship and ministry that are relevant—and therefore comfortable—to their cultural perceptions.

Having been raised in the traditional church, I would have been happy to sing hymns and sit in pews for the rest of my life. But after discovering most unchurched people want a fresh break from these old-fashioned forms, I determined to mold my church into one where the average unchurched person would feel very comfortable with the surroundings.

Likewise, Wally's objective is to ensure that the message of the cross is the only thing that might offend an unchurched person entering his church's worship services. Paul said it this way:

> So whether you eat or drink or whatever you do, do it all for the glory of God. Do not cause anyone to stumble, whether Jews, Greeks, or the church of God—even as I try to please everybody in every way. For I am not seeking my own good but the good of many, so that they may be saved.
>
> 1 Corinthians 10:31–33

The contemporary versus traditional question will be particularly crucial in specific cultural settings. In some midwestern small towns, a pastor who tried to introduce a contemporary worship service might be tarred and feathered. But the opposite is true in a city like San Francisco. Pastor Michael Brodeur of Vineyard Christian Fellowship told me:

> Culturally, sociologically, and spiritually San Francisco is a place of escape from traditional values. The city is probably one of the world's ten worst propagators of godless trends and subcultures. Churches have had great difficulty here, with the largest having only six hundred people and several others having fewer than four hundred people. Those who have transplanted Christianity here have tried to do it with the same language and style of the traditional places from which people have run away.

Most church plantings have failed because these churches have put their resources into easily identifiable target groups which don't make good disciples—singling out gays, the homeless, or AIDS victims. They exhaust their resources on a very difficult base of return and sabotage their own ministry.

Reflecting on the success of Vineyard Christian Fellowship in San Francisco, Brodeur added:

We came in determined not to target these groups, but just to go after the average person. At first our attenders were not from the city but from outlying areas, which was a strategy of God to get us over the initial growth and financial barriers of establishing a church in the heart of the city. Now 70 percent of our attenders are city residents.

Brodeur recognized that, because of cultural restraints, his church's first issue was to *broaden* its target audience. "We couldn't let the usual constraints restrain us," he said. "In San Francisco, because of the car, the neighborhood church no longer exists." But in other churches with other cultural settings, the reverse might be true, and the strategy employed by Vineyard might be a recipe for disaster.

Vineyard represents the importance of viewing a church through the cultural composition of a target audience. We must ask ourselves: "Is our failure to multiply an adequate number of culturally diverse types of churches preventing anyone from coming to Christ?" If so—and I suspect that the answer is a very definite yes—we may find ourselves subject to some stern warnings in Scripture. One warning issued by Christ himself deals specifically in the context of causing believing children to sin, but we can apply the principle to anyone who finds himself a victim of our lack of obedience to the Great Commission:

But if anyone causes one of these little ones who believe in me to sin, it would be better for him to have a large millstone hung around his neck and to be drowned in the depths of the sea. Woe to the world because of the things that cause people to sin! Such things must come, but woe to the man through whom they come!

Matthew 18:6, 7

In many cases the first issue your church may have to deal with, if it desires to be culturally relevant, is the sign on your front lawn. Your church name says a great deal about the culture to which you are appealing. If it includes a denominational or culturally charged word, you will appeal only to those who identify with that denomination or who don't know any better.

Both Cynthia Henseler and her husband had come from traditional church backgrounds, but had concluded that organized religion was unnecessary and that they should be self-sufficient Christians. Lee was an upwardly mobile professional. They were well-educated, in their early thirties and new parents who wanted to provide their daughter with good Christian values.

Though they had given up on religion, they were attracted by the vision for a new church presented in a letter they received from a young local pastor named Rick Warren. They began to attend the new church, Saddleback Valley Community Church, and found it comfortable and enjoyable. They were surprised to find a religious organization that actually was culturally relevant to their own lives.

In the eight years since they began to attend, both Cynthia and her husband have come to know the Lord and are serving him faithfully in the church. Cynthia, who now is director of women's ministries, reflects, "If we had known when we first came that this was a 'Baptist' church, we never would have set foot in the door." Fortunately, Warren had strategically chosen a "neutral" name in order to reach out beyond those with a Baptist background.

It was for this very reason that Bethany Baptist Church of Long Beach recently took the word *Baptist* out of its name. Pastor Dennis Beatty, convinced that they would be more effective if they marketed themselves so that their Baptist heritage was low-key, says, "For a church that had an eighty-year history with the same name, changing it was like tampering with the Gospel." But he worked with the elders for many months until they all had ownership of the change, and they haven't regretted it.

We have structured too many churches for the sake and comfort of those who already are Christians and are attending them, rather than for the sake of those people who are unchurched. Frank Tillapaugh calls this "the fortress mentality." Church members without question assume that the church exists to meet their needs, and they therefore structure their programs and build their facility with that in mind. Of the many churches with gymnasiums on their premises, how many do you know that use it as a tool of outreach—sponsoring community games, local events, and unchurched athletic teams—and how many use it for the relaxation and pleasure of the church's members?

If such a church suddenly reorients its focus to meeting the needs of the unchurched, members often will turn on the pressure with such statements as "we're not getting enough meat in the worship services."

Tillapaugh's solution to this problem was not to *replace* traditional worship services, but to *add* a contemporary service. "It would have been very difficult for us to change any of the four traditional services on Sunday morning to adopt this approach," he said. "Instead, we simply rented a junior high school auditorium and started another service at 11:15 A.M. on Sunday. We began with the same ingredients [as Willow Creek Community Church and Saddleback Community Church]—band, drama team, and basic, relevant preaching. On August 2, 1987, 175 people, nearly all of them from our church, showed up the first Sunday. We now [as of Spring 1988] have around 300 attending, and we know of about 20 who have prayed to receive Christ."[2]

Pastor Rick Warren determined to reach unchurched people when he founded Saddleback Valley Community Church in Mission Viejo, California. "First we looked all around us and asked the question, 'Why are so many traditional churches not growing?' " he recalls. From the beginning they decided to be "a church for the unchurched. No matter how much pressure people put on us, we will always be that," he says. Warren's church is on the flip side of the coin from Tillapaugh's—rather than add a contemporary service to their traditional services, he has considered adding a traditional service to their many contemporary services.

Among the crucial decisions a church must make is what it desires to accomplish during its public worship services. Is your primary purpose to edify church members, to train them, or to evangelize and assimilate the unchurched? Most churches attempt a combination of all these, though the primary focus is on edifying and training church members. Lip service may be paid to the need for evangelism by issuing an altar call at the end of the sermon, but very little thought is given to activities that might assimilate the unchurched.

Saddleback Valley is an outstanding example of a church that gears its public worship services to the unchurched. The church attracts newcomers with star performers who are highly advertised in the community during several special days each year. Once visitors arrive, Saddleback Valley treats them to its unique mix of uplifting, contemporary chorus singing and the simple but dynamic teaching of Pastor Warren.

It's astounding how many churches, rather than trying to make their services inviting and comfortable for the unchurched newcomer, actually do the opposite. Take, for example, the practice of forcing visitors to stand up at some point in a worship service so that your church's scalp-hungry regular attenders may ogle them appreciatively. The unchurched newcomer driven to a church because of a glaring lack in his or her life does not particularly want to be singled out and put on public display. Being issued a big, red badge that says VISITOR may have the same effect. Bill Hybels, pastor of one of the country's most successful churches for the unchurched, Willow Creek Community Church near Chicago, says he does everything in his power to ensure a visitor's anonymity while allowing people the freedom to respond when they are ready to do so.

CBC recently decided to gear its five public worship services more intentionally to meet the needs of the unchurched. This meant more skits, drama, and other creative forms of communication; a greater dependence upon quality musicianship and uplifting, easy-to-sing choruses; and continued focus on simple but dynamic teaching by Rob Acker, who is an evangelist and knows how to speak the language of the unchurched. CBC strives for an appropriate balance of quality for believers that is "seeker sensitive."

Previous to this, under my leadership, we already had designated the last two Sunday-morning services as being intended more for the unchurched. We encouraged our faithful attenders and members to move to any of the other three services and vacate their seats for newcomers. We discovered that these two late services on Sunday morning were the ones that were most frequented by the unchurched, but members also liked them, so they were the most crowded.

We discovered that being full (which I will define as having more than 80 percent of the available seating, children's Bible class, or parking space filled) was as effective a way to turn away the unchurched as putting out a FOR MEMBERS ONLY sign. The primary way that God needed to grow our congregation was by helping us see the need to expand our facility in order to more readily accommodate the unchurched. But even a short time after we did this—moving our regular attenders to alternate services, increasing our parking, increasing our children's Bible class space with temporary modular buildings, and even knocking out one wall in the church to expand auditorium seating—we once again were confronted with the challenge of more effectively attracting and assimilating the unchurched in our weekend worship services.

Look carefully at the ways your church attracts and assimilates the unchurched. Is the public worship service an important vehicle in your church for accomplishing that function, as it is in most churches? Then you'll want to consider carefully the cultural aspects of **every** part of that public worship service to ensure that it promotes and does not hinder the unchurched person's acceptance of the Gospel message.

In the ideal church of the coming decades, what Ralph Neighbour calls the cell-group church and Carl George terms the metachurch, assimilation of the unchurched will occur through the *side door*—that is, through the unchurched person's involvement in a church's cell groups (invited by a neighbor, friend, or relative who is a member of both the church and the cell group) or through fishing-pool activities such as special seminars to which the community is invited, and designed to give them exposure to the church's life. This contrasts with assimilation through the *front door*—the public worship service. But as long as the front door still is the main entrance for so many into the church, we'll have to think very carefully about what our public worship services incorporate to attract and hold unchurched people.

The cost of being a church for the unchurched may not only be internal pressure from your members, but external pressure as well. When CBC first began, those who were watching us—primarily other churches in our denomination which had an interest in our church because of their financial support or the loan made by the denomination—very rapidly realized that we were becoming a church that was somewhat different from their expectations. The first thing that bothered them was our refusal to pass an offering basket during our formative years. This gave them the perception that we were fiscally irresponsible, when in reality our call for financial responsibility of our members was much more rigorous than their own. They also were concerned that we sang so many popular choruses, rather than the old hymns, and that we used contemporary instruments such as guitars, synthesizers, and drums. (Saddleback Community Church uses bongos!)

But the straw which finally broke the camel's back was when someone from one of these other churches happened upon a CBC softball team at a picnic in the park, celebrating after winning a game. This person perceived a few of these men to be drinking beer, and so the word quickly spread that CBC was the "beer-drinking church."

The busybodies who reported this apparently weren't aware that we designed our softball teams primarily as an outreach "bridge" activity to the unchurched, and that the "offenders" sitting in the park that day were unbelievers (who, by the way, were attracted to our church as a result of playing on our softball team and later became Christians).

So I suppose that we were at fault for not cracking down and letting the unchurched know that if they wanted to associate with us, they would have to quit doing things which made us uncomfortable. I'm sure if Christ had done the same, instead of eating and drinking with sinners and tax collectors, we'd have no problem following his example. As it is, however, we'll have to content ourselves with being "the beer-drinking church." Sigh. Nothing like suffering for Jesus, eh?

The Gentile Jew

The quotation from 1 Corinthians 9 at the beginning of this chapter proves the importance of the principle of using a flexible method adapted to fit the culture of your target group. Paul did not find it in any way incongruous to adapt the way he presents himself in order to appropriate and effectively communicate his acultural Gospel message.

One of my most enjoyable experiences since joining the staff of Church Resource Ministries is the time I have spent with John Hayes. John is a sophisticated and brilliant Princeton/Yale graduate who directs CRM's InnerChange ministry, a division of the organization that targets the urban poor. One of his goals is to develop cell-group churches among Cambodian refugees packed into rows of squalid apartments in Santa Ana, California's, infamous Minnie Street.

As you wheel your car onto Minnie Street from the nicely manicured suburban thoroughfare which intersects it, the world suddenly is transformed. The shabby apartments are bursting at the seams with refugees. People are everywhere; young men stand listlessly on the street corners; drug deals go down openly on the streets and in parked cars; children run nearly naked on the asphalt, even when it rains. People congregate between the buildings where they cook meals over open fires—many don't have utilities in their homes—or hang their laundry to dry. As I walked into John's apartment in the middle of all this, my presence brought many suspicious stares. I nervously noted bullet holes in the walls. I never felt so much like a WASP in all my life.

The first thing I noticed about John's apartment is the lack of furniture. His bedroll is on the floor, where he sleeps oblivious to the roaches and other scuttling night creatures. He has spruced up his paint-chipped walls with pictures drawn by young Cambodians who attend his Bible classes. His books are stacked unceremoniously in various corners of the room.

The occasion for this particular visit was a CRM strategic planning meeting. CRM's president, Sam Metcalf, picked up John's chalkboard and propped it against one wall, and we all pulled up a seat—on the floor—and began.

John is a young, articulate Christian leader. He has a mind like a can opener and proceeded to use it to remove the lid from some of our preconceived notions about the inner-city poor. Listening to him, lost in the challenge of the good-natured give-and-take, I marvelled at his sophisticated brilliance.

When it was time for a break, we mustered our courage and asked John for a tour of the neighborhood. *Just this once*, he said, since he didn't want to be seen too often hanging around white people who had *vice squad* written all over their faces.

Then it happened. John put on a black Levi jacket, combed back his hair a certain way, and sauntered out the door. Suddenly he was *one of them*.

The Princeton sophisticate and missions strategist had the look, the lingo, even the streetwise swagger. He certainly was convincing! Just walking next to him made me very nervous.

John is studying hard—even to the point of learning the difficult Cambodian dialect still spoken by most of the refugees—and adapting himself as completely as possible to the ghetto culture of those God has called him to reach.

When Paul was with Jews, he was himself. He wore Jewish clothes, ate Jewish food, observed Jewish customs, and used Jewish forms of communication. But when he was with Gentiles, he was someone else. Among the Greeks, he adapted fully to their cultural style, even employing their method of debate in his communication. Hypocritical? Not at all. The essence of his message never changed.

John's message now is the same as Paul's was then: In spite of all the trouble you've been through, God loves you. He shed his own blood to save you. He wants to take your life and make you a new creature.

The goal of this strategy is simply effective evangelism—"that I might win some." Paul recognizes that, even with this strategy and the full blessing of the Lord, he's not going to win everyone. But he sure is going to try to win as many as possible. This is the nature of running the race.

What do most Americans hold as their dearest possession? The answer is clear—their freedom. Yet Paul was so convinced of the importance of his goal of effective evangelism that he gladly gave up even his freedom—his freedom to be the kind of person he was most comfortable being.

Doubtless John Hayes, with his sharp mind and sociological training, would be most comfortable with a six-digit salary, advising some multinational corporation how to work successfully in a cross-cultural situation. But John willingly has given up his freedom to achieve that type of life-style, and has opted instead to sleep on the floor and risk his life planting churches on Minnie Street. All for the sake of the Gospel.

You see, being culturally relevant is actually another way of describing what incarnating the Gospel is all about. It means putting good news into forms that relate and communicate to people where they are. Of course the best example of this is what God did in the ultimate incarnation, when he himself became man in Jesus Christ. Cultural relevance means incarnational ministry, of which John Hayes is an excellent twentieth-century example.

In every culture, *commitment to the people*, although it may be manifested in different forms, is part of the sacrifice that you must make as a church planter. Tom Nebel discovered that in the rural community of Whitewater, Wisconsin, one of the keys to the success of his growing church was sending an important message to the community that he was there to stay.

"When I bought a house," he told me, "the congregation breathed a sigh of relief. They were watching and judging to see whether I was serious about this adventure." Discovery of this principle truly paid for itself, however, when the young church started thinking about permanent facilities. "Someone suggested classified ads saying we were looking for land. It was a brilliant strategy for a small town." They were leveling off at about 120 people, but when they began to communicate to the community that they were serious about staying and committing themselves to the people of Whitewater, the attendance began climbing sharply.

The Importance of *Naive Listening*

To be a "Gentile to the Gentiles" brings to the forefront the importance of *listening* to the people you are trying to reach. What are their felt needs? What barriers are preventing them from responding to the Gospel? I firmly believe that a leader should not start a church without at least an informal opinion survey, and then a comprehensive demographic survey of the target community.[3]

John Sculley, chief executive officer of Apple Computers, has claimed that "no great marketing decisions have ever been made on quantitative data" alone. In his book, *Thriving on Chaos*, Tom Peters devotes much space to help executives develop their listening skills, because:

> After years of dealing with managers beset by turbulent conditions, my correspondence from police chiefs, mayors, school principals, hospital administrators, and businesspersons occupies many a file cabinet. The most moving letters by far are the hundreds about "simple listening." In fact, if I had a file labeled "religious conversion"—that is, correspondence from those whose management practices have truly been transformed—I would suspect that 50 percent of its contents would deal with just one, narrow topic: going out anew, with a "naive" mind-set, and listening to customers. (Another 25 or so percent would be from managers who had done the same thing with their people—another version of "naive" listening.)[4]

Asserting that most new product ideas already exist in customers' minds and practical needs, and are waiting for someone to listen and act, Peters suggests three components to this listening process: "Listening to customers must become everyone's business. Listening means: (1) hanging out (on their turf), (2) listening naively and with intensity, and (3) providing fast feedback and taking action."[5]

The immediate goal of naive listening is getting to know your target group. It is helpful to visualize a personification representing precisely whom it is you want to reach. Bill Hybels calls this personification Unchurched Harry; Rick Warren's name for this nebulous character is Saddleback Sam. Warren describes Saddleback Sam with astonishing precision:

> . . . a young urban professional with some religious background as a child, who hasn't been to church for 15 or 20 years. He is affluent and recreation conscious. He is interested in health, but is stressed-out. He is usually against organized religion. He doesn't want to be recognized when he comes to church. And, he is self-satisfied.[6]

As you conduct interviews with unchurched people in your target community, build a composite picture of your own Unchurched Harry. Why doesn't Unchurched Harry (or Harriet) go to church? What would it take to get him or her there? What type of teaching, what subject matter, what type of music, what type of atmosphere will attract him? What type of relationship would a neighbor or friend who is a member of your church need to cultivate with this person before he would be tempted to come? What type of special event might draw him there? You can ask a myriad of questions to help you form a picture of your Unchurched Harry.

Developing Your Philosophy

One of the greatest mistakes in planting a church is beginning with the assumption that it will be a church for everybody. No church can serve everybody. Every successful church has a unique angle, something special to offer to a particular population segment. Every successful church planter realizes that the principle of affinity—that people will attract and be attracted by those who are culturally similar to themselves—profoundly influences what their church will look like.

Rick Warren explains, "It takes all kinds of churches to reach all kinds of people." Your philosophy-of-ministry statement is your guiding light in determining what kind of church you are going to be, based on what kind of people you desire to attract.

Your starting point is selecting a target group. This relates back to the vision that the Lord has given you. Specifically what kind of people are you burdened to reach?

Keep in mind that your chances for success will be greatest when people who are culturally just like you comprise the largest part of your target group. Perhaps, like John Hayes, you have that cross-cultural gift which allows you to build a bridge between your own culture and the culture of those you are burdened to reach. However, most of us simply do not have this gift. Yet if we look hard enough, we can identify a group of people who are culturally very similar in composition to ourselves, yet who have a distinct need for a growing and reproducing church.

Once your church of culturally similar people has been established, you will want to look carefully at how you can plant new churches among distinct ethnic or other culturally different groups from your own. Chapter 10 deals more with this idea.

Because of these sociological realities, most seminary or graduate school professionals attract white collar populations more readily than blue collar. Yet there is a tremendous need for churches among blue collar populations. As church leadership is raised up increasingly through the rank and file of growing churches, rather than through the halls of academia, this disparity will be addressed.

Tom Nebel struggled with this as he began planting his church. Though in a rural part of the nation, Whitewater itself is a college town, but small and countryfied, "like Sam Drucker in Hooterville," Tom says. Therefore both white and blue collar people worship together in the same church.

"I now can tell within five minutes if we will assimilate someone walking in the door," Tom says. "Usually it's an issue of whether that person is attracted to my personality." Tom says that at first he put much energy into assimilating the blue collars attending the church, but it didn't pay off. "I even went coon hunting with them," Tom says. He believes the blue collars easily are intimidated by the white collars, and never would invite one over for dinner. The blue collars eventually bonded to one of the elders, but it is tenuous whether or not the entire group will remain with the church.

With his seminary education, Tom realizes now he might have been better off to target white collars from the beginning. "But in such a small town," he says, "the reality is that you're happy to have anyone who walks through the door."

The issue, though, is not that you are going to deflect or send away those who do not fit your desired target audience. It is, rather, whom will you structure your church to attract? If you structure your church to attract blue collars, and white collars come, God bless 'em. But recognize that God has called you to put your time and energy into assimilating and developing the blue collars (or whatever is the description of your intended target audience), and don't apologize for it. This is the reason for having a *written* philosophy of ministry, so everyone can understand why you are favoring one type of person over another in the way you spend your time and energy. Effective pastors realize that their church in a socioculturally complex society must be a *specialist*, rather than a generalist.

After defining your target audience, you must determine their felt needs.

Whoa! Just a minute, you say. *This is beginning to sound too much like marketing to me and not enough like church. Isn't this watering down the Gospel?*

If it is, then Christ was as guilty as any of us. He recognized that if you don't meet people at the point of their felt needs, you will have no opportunity to address their real and more significant spiritual need.

Why did Christ risk precious time discussing water, politics, and religion with the Samaritan woman at the well? Christ addressed her at the point of her felt needs—and his strategy was effective, as shown by her plea: "Sir, give me this water so that I won't get thirsty and have to keep coming here to draw water" (John 4:15). She was still on a physical rather than a spiritual plane. Christ knew that after their conversation she would have to continue coming to the well to draw water to meet her physical needs. Was he deceiving her? No, he simply was using her felt need to create a bridge to her real spiritual need. If he simply had said, "Now, listen to these four spiritual laws. Law one—God loves you and has a wonderful plan for your life," the woman would have given him a strange look and gone quickly about her business . . . and eventually to hell.

This is not watering down the Gospel in the least; it is creating opportunities to present it. I remember opening a fortune cookie once which wisely said, "You must begin from where you are; you cannot start from anywhere else." We have no magic transporter beam; we must make and cross our bridges in order to reach our destination. Ministry is simply the process of taking people from where they are now and leading them to where they need to be.

This is beginning a written philosophy-of-ministry statement, which I will help guide you through in the next section. Just as the process of listening is dynamic and not static, your philosophy-of-ministry statement must be a dynamic document, refined constantly as your ministry progresses. (Chalk up one more good reason to have a word processor!)

In his best-selling book, *Future Shock,* author Alvin Toffler very dramatically illustrates the nature of change and the impact it will have on our futures.[7] He shows not only how technology and society themselves are changing, but even how the rate of change is changing. It is increasing exponentially. This means more change has occurred in the last thirty years than during all of history before it, and chances are that more change will occur in the next ten years than in the last thirty.

As the future unfolds, you will find the needs of your target audience to be forever in flux, and the listening process will have no ending point. I recommend that church planters and pastors retake their entire survey every three years to stay on top of the needs of their target communities.

Rick Warren's Saddleback Valley parishioners agree that one of Rick's greatest strengths is his ability to listen to people. He asks people continually, "What do you perceive your needs to be?" Through his church chats he continues to sample the unchurched entering the doors of his church in order to determine what brought them and what will keep them there.

The philosophical transitions evident upon reading Tom Peters's most recent book, *Thriving on Chaos,* in contrast to his previous book, the best-selling "Bible of business management," *In Search of Excellence,* are fascinating. He has undergone, as a result of this changing rate of change that Toffler postulates, a major philosophical shift from "Figure out what you do best and systematize it" to "Figure out how you can adapt your organization to roll with the punches and stay on top of an everchanging market."

The successful church of the twenty-first century and beyond will be one that learns how to listen to people, establishes a culturally relevant philosophy of ministry, and adapts its ministry strategies to their ever-changing needs.

Action Steps

Identify your target group

What type of people has God given you a burden to reach?

What type of people would respond best to your leadership?

Make a commitment before the Lord that you will strive to fill your church with lost sheep (unchurched unbelievers) and stray sheep (unchurched believers), not just Christians who already are churched. Too many churches pad their rolls with the Christians who shuffle from church to church. Ironically, while attracting disgruntled Christians presents a tempting way to boost growth initially, it is often because of the sort of person who is unwilling to commit his loyalty to a church that these churches begin to decay.

Cultivate your passion for listening.

Listen both objectively and subjectively for facts and for perceptions. Listen naively.

Try a variety of listening methods. Plan several ways to connect with the people in your church and community.

Take a walking survey of your community, if you've never done so, or if you haven't done so for three years. Robert Schuller suggests pastors block two weeks in their schedule during which they do not have any appointments or other commitments, including preaching. Spend the time knocking on doors, simply listening to the needs of the unchurched. Says Schuller, "It will revolutionize your ministry."

Take your pen (or your word processor) in hand and describe your philosophy of ministry in one or two paragraphs. There is no set format for doing this; it simply may be a description of your Unchurched Harry or Saddleback Sam and how you will structure your worship, programs, and ministry to meet this person's needs.

Your *philosophy of ministry* should help you define your *style* of ministry, which is your distinctive approach to ministry that will give your church its unique personality. This will aid you as you determine areas of growth. It will act as a screen upon which you will base your acceptance of new ministries or elimination of ineffective ones. In short, it will help you more fully reach the unchurched.

After you have written it, apply these tests to your philosophy of ministry:

Does it state . . .

What it is about our church that makes us unique?

What type of person are we seeking to reach?

Is it accurate to your experience?

Is it stated in a manner that is:

Accurate?

Enduring?

Succinct?

Memorable?

Believable?

Energizing to all?

A philosophy of ministry example that I enjoy citing is CRM's slogan: "Serving and extending the church worldwide."

Work toward the point where everyone in the organization can understand and state its uniqueness (strategic distinction in the marketplace) in twenty-five words or less. According to Peters, this ability is a benchmark by which to test organizational ownership of your vision as your philosophy of ministry expresses it.

Notes

1. Developed by Robert Schuller and Rick Warren.

2. *The Unleashing Connection* (Spring 1988), p. 3.

3. Extensive guidance on how to conduct an effective demographic survey is available in the *Church Planting Workbook*, coauthored by Bob Logan and Jeff Rast and available from Charles E. Fuller Institute.

4. Tom Peters, *Thriving on Chaos* (New York: Alfred A. Knopf, 1987), p. 149.

5. Ibid., pp. 144, 150.

6. Sherri Brown, "The Search for Saddleback Sam," *Missions USA* (July-August 1988), pp. 13–14.

7. Alvin Toffler, *Future Shock* (New York: Random House, 1970), pp. 20ff.

Principle 4

Celebrative and Reflective Worship

Come, let us bow down in worship, let us kneel before the Lord our Maker; for he is our God and we are the people of his pasture, the flock under his care.

Psalm 95:6, 7

I have learned a great deal about the nature of genuine worship from my friend and colleague Byron Spradlin, who is executive director of Artists in Christian Testimony and senior pastor of a CBC daughter church, New Hope Church in Rancho Cucamonga, California. Byron defines *worship* as "an active response to the person and work of God." He says that New Hope's goal in worship is "to inspire unchurched people in a way that they would feel that they have met with God."

People who attend New Hope make many positive comments about their church: "For the first time in my life, I'm enjoying and looking forward to coming to church. I feel so comfortable. I love the music! For the first time in a church I feel I can get close to God."

Due to its multidimensional nature, worship is as deep and complex a subject as one can tackle. We sometimes view worship as an activity with physical manifestation, yet Jesus told the Samaritan woman at the well," . . . a time is coming and has now come when the true worshipers will worship the Father in spirit and truth, for they are the kind of worshipers the Father seeks. God is spirit, and his worshipers must worship in spirit and in truth" (John 4:23, 24).

What does it mean to worship *in spirit and in truth*? Is worship a mystical art, attainable only to those who have achieved some sort of evangelical nirvana? Are there clear and easy steps that you can point to and say, "Do these things and you will be worshiping God"?

While we were conducting research for this book we asked pastors of large and growing churches to define and evaluate their church's worship and the extent to which it could be characterized by each of the following qualities:

76

Celebrative	Reflective
Grand and sweeping	Fun
Comfortable	Sorrowful or repentant
Interactive	Planned/structured
Flexible/sensitive to the Holy Spirit	

Celebrative and *planned/structured* received the most consistently high marks, followed by *reflective* and *flexible/sensitive to the Holy Spirit*.

Paradoxes of Worship

The variety of responses and the paradoxical nature of some of the characteristics receiving equally high marks (*celebrative* versus *reflective*, and *planned/structured* versus *flexible/sensitive* to the Holy Spirit) reflects the dynamic, complex, and multidimensional nature of true worship. A worship event takes people through a process of response to God which recognizes:

Who God is and what he is like.
Who we are in relation to him and what we are like.
The change that he desires to bring to our life.
Our proper response to his will for our life.

Worship has many multidimensional facets.

An Activity Versus a State of Being

Worship most commonly is thought and spoken of as an *activity.* "At this," said John near the end of his revelation, "I fell at his feet to worship him . . . " (Revelation 19:10). Worship is something that you do at a given point in time, and stop doing at another given point in time. But worship also is a state of being, a lifelong activity. This is similar to Paul's command to "pray continually" (1 Thessalonians 5:17), thus making prayer a state of being, even though prayer more commonly is regarded as an activity. "Worship the Lord your God," the Lord dictated to Moses on Mount Sinai, "and his blessing will be on your food and water. I will take away sickness from among you, and none will miscarry or be barren in your land. I will give you a full life span" (Exodus 23:25, 26). Here the word *worship* alternately is translated as "serve," shedding insight on the nature of worship as a state of being. To worship God as a lifelong occupation is to be devoted to serving him.

Pastoral leaders must have an experience and commitment to the true and dynamic worship of God in their own lives before they can lead God's people in worship. Worship must describe the state of being of their lives as well as a regular activity in which they participate. Scripture shows that worship both precedes and produces ministry. Before being sent to pharaoh on behalf of the children of Israel, Moses was called to worship the *I AM* before the burning bush: " 'Do not come any closer,' God said. 'Take off your sandals, for the place where you are standing is holy ground' " (Exodus 3:5). Isaiah's experience of heavenly worship, where the superlative seraphim stood above the throne of God and called to one another, " . . . Holy, holy, holy is the Lord Almighty; the whole earth is full of his glory" preceded his call from the Lord: "Then I heard the voice of the Lord saying, 'Whom shall I send? And who will go for us?' and I said, 'Here am I. Send me!' " (Isaiah 6:3, 8). And the eleven disciples worshiped at the feet of Christ immediately before he delivered that famous assignment, "Therefore go and make disciples of all nations, baptizing them in the name of the Father and of the Son and of the Holy Spirit, and teaching them to obey everything I have commanded you. And surely I am with you always, to the very end of the age" (Matthew 28:19, 20).

Sadly, in the vast majority of evangelical churches, if the worship component were alive, it would be on the critical list. Most unbelievers justifiably perceive worship in the average church as dull, boring, and irrelevant. The shame of this situation is that quality worship is so vital not only to the spiritual life of believers within a church, but also to the church's ability to attract and assimilate the unchurched.

As a pastor, if you desire true worship of the living God to be released among the people of your congregation, such worship first must first be released in your own life and in your own worship patterns before your congregation.

Personal Versus Corporate

Worship is an intensely personal activity or state of being. We worship God from the innermost part of our being. Even if you are worshiping in the midst of a large crowd, whether they are dear friends or complete strangers, in order to truly worship you must lose the part of yourself that manages your social interaction with others—the part that worries about what kind of an impression you will make. You must be completely free to be transparent before the throne of God, to allow his Spirit that lives within you to express the dynamic and the devotion to his lordship that Paul suggests: ". . . the Spirit himself intercedes for us with groans that words cannot express" (Romans 8:26).

Although worship can be a personal activity you can engage in while driving on the freeway, worship at its best is a corporate activity during which the diverse gifts and the interplay of a body of believers committed to exalting Christ and hearing from God creates a dynamic that lifts the individual believer to new heights. Worship is keenly sensitive to environment, to the mood established by music, lighting, the testimony of others, and the reading of Scripture. Yet true worship can occur even deep in a black, rat-infested, stench-ridden prison cell, as Paul and Silas so amply demonstrated in Acts 16:25.

Celebrative Versus Reflective

The balance between celebration and reflection is absolutely essential to healthy worship. Most churches err to one side or the other, and usually to the *reflective* side; their worship is morose, self-flagellating, and humdrum—what I call the such-a-worm-as-I syndrome. Yet other churches err on the *celebrative* side. Their worship is nothing but happy, happy, happy, and never gives participants the opportunity to reflect upon their relationship with God or to grieve over their sins.

True worship is not a static activity, but a dynamic process of receiving vision from God. It's important that those who lead the body of Christ—those whom the body depends upon to a great extent for its vision—be among the best at worshiping God.

When God gives vision, he first reveals to believers something about his own nature. This revelation evokes a variety of responses in the believer, some of which are almost antithetical.

We see in Moses, as God's person was revealed to him, an exultance, a radiance, and a great joy. This revelation to Moses was so intense that his very flesh glowed—literally, physically glowed—after he stood in God's presence. He was divinely irradiated (Exodus 34:29).

On the other hand, we see in Isaiah another legitimate reaction to the revelation of God's person. Isaiah was so dismayed at the presence of God that he cried out, "Woe to me! . . . I am ruined! For I am a man of unclean lips, and I live among a people of unclean lips, and my eyes have seen the King, the Lord Almighty" (Isaiah 6:5). Likewise, Ezekiel fell to his face like a dead man before the presence of the Lord, full of terror evoked by the absolute majesty of a God who " . . . lives in unapproachable light . . . " (1 Timothy 6:16; *see also* Ezekiel 1:28).

Such undoneness results when God impresses upon us the reality of our own sinfulness in contrast to his own holiness. The vision that God gives enables us to see clearly not only his perfect character, but also our own corruption. Thus, one aspect of the process of worship will be a *reflection* upon our own lives, that searching and cleansing process that allows God's Holy Spirit to illumine our hearts and expose what he finds there. Having to deal with our sin in the presence of a holy God brings both grief and joy.

In *The Great Divorce*, the master storyteller C. S. Lewis tells of a man who is visiting heaven and is plagued by a lizard that sits upon his shoulder and whispers unwholesome things into his ear. The angel who is to accompany the man upon his tour of heaven urges the man to allow him to pick the lizard off his shoulder and break its back. The man is terrified; even though he is tormented by the lizard and would love to be free of it, he has lived so long under its influence that he fears what might happen to him if it were removed.

Eventually the angel persists, and the writhing lizard is snatched away and its back broken. The man screams in a moment of agony, but then is flushed with relief and joy as the holy river of God washes away the stain of sin.

These conflicting emotions are similar to what happens in the process of the true worship of God. Many times people fear worship; they hold back, hesitant at what they see and don't know. They inwardly fear the pain of letting go of themselves and allowing God free rein.

And yet, quality, dynamic worship is one of the most attractive forces in the growing church. The popularity and power of the charismatic renewal movement is due in part to its focus upon the emotional and spiritual cathartic of the dynamic worship process. A very definite correlation exists between well-planned and vital worship and the ability of a church to communicate positive and meaningful Christianity to the unchurched.

Several years ago at CBC, God started to work among us so that we realized the necessity of learning to express the desire of our hearts in worship. Since our denominational background is quite conservative and nondemonstrative, we wondered how best to release those inhibitions holding back our congregation from being more expressive in worship. By expressive I'm referring merely to a more active worship in which many of the worship-related activities in the Psalms and elsewhere in Scripture are happening in our congregation, rather than simple, passive singing or listening. These activities include lifting hands and faces unto the Lord; clapping hands; bowing down low before him and weeping over our sinfulness and inadequacy; singing and shouting for joy; playing a variety of musical instruments; and perhaps even dancing in exultation before him, as David did before the ark of the covenant (1 Chronicles 15:29). We decided not only to profile in our teaching the need for more expressive worship, but also to model it boldly ourselves.

Since we generally sit in the front row during worship activities, with several hundred people at our backs, initially I found this to be quite a personal challenge. But as I began to allow the joy of the Lord to flood and control my spirit, I was released to worship him in truth, and soon it no longer mattered what those around me were doing or what they were thinking. I was free to allow my father's advice more fully, to find out what the Lord wanted me to do—in worship—and to do it.

This doesn't mean that you can't worship the Lord in quietness. At times, worship will call for silence. This is just one facet of healthy worship. It's like attending a major sporting event. If you're at a college football game, at times it may be appropriate to reflect quietly upon what is happening (particularly if your team is losing sorely—or perhaps if your favorite player just was carried off the field on a stretcher). However, if you are quiet and glum throughout the entire game, your fellow sports enthusiasts will begin to think that something is missing in your capacity to enjoy a good sporting event the way it was meant to be enjoyed—with shouting, cheers, laughter, and jumping up from one's seat; in short, with energy and enthusiasm.

The raw fact is that most of us find it far easier to get excited about our favorite sports team than about worshiping the Most High God. Yet a great multitude of adoring saints in the Revelation of John fall upon their faces before the throne of God and cry out with a loud voice, "Salvation belongs to our God, who sits on the throne, and to the Lamb. . . . Amen! Praise and glory and wisdom and thanks and honor and power and strength be to our God for ever and ever. Amen!" (Revelation 7:10, 12).

How much more demonstrative ought we to be in the presence of such a Holy One than in the presence of our favorite sports team? I am convinced that if we examine our lives and find that we get more excited about anything else (how about winning the lottery?) than we get about worshiping God, then perhaps he is not number one in our lives.

It is important to distinguish between reflective worship and worship that is morose. Silence has a definite place in worship. While lecturing in New Zealand recently, I was discussing the dynamics of worship with an Anglican sister. Admitting that their style of worship was quite reserved, she said, "I never could be a Pentecostal. I think their high energy worship would wear me out." I began to understand that different personality types, who display their celebrative feelings in different ways, naturally may congregate in certain types of churches or denominations which employ different levels or types of worship participation.

The Psalmist quoted, "Be still, and know that I am God . . . " (46:10). Meditation, reflection, and quiet confession all are an important part of the worship process.

Not everyone in our congregation yet feels comfortable raising their hands, let alone dancing in the aisle. Some even don't feel comfortable singing. As a result of the pastors' modeling this positive behavior, enough people have been released to worship God the way God wants them to, and it no longer is a spectacle or an issue. After involvement in so much passive, joyless worship all these years, my heart is greatly encouraged finally to see people being freed to worship God *actively* and *joyfully*.

The worship process employed by New Song Church in Pomona, California, even though it is a very young church, has been a great example to me of this balance of celebration and reflection which contributes to healthy worship. New Song's musically gifted pastor, Dieter Zander, starts the service in a high energy mode, grabbing focus and erasing stray thoughts. From celebration they move into a time of reflection, during which people are left standing in the presence of God, confronted by his holiness and their own inadequacies. This process prepares the congregation for the teaching from the Word which follows. After personal application and the challenge to respond to what the Holy Spirit desires to do in their lives, they again move into a celebrative mode. The worship service ends with everyone leaving feeling very good about meeting with God and being touched by him.

I recognize that it is particularly difficult for pastors to acquire an attitude of true worship. The back of your mind is always on the details of environment, transition, and so on. You necessarily are focused on management of the service rather than on the worship you are trying to facilitate. Entering into worship under these circumstances is a discipline and a skill that takes time and experience to develop, and it may not happen overnight. Yet the sooner you are released to worship God in spirit and truth, the sooner your people will begin to respond to him.

Meanwhile, *how* do you prevent worship from going stale? How do you inject into it that celebrative and reflective life and vitality so desperately needed by churches today?

Characteristics of Vital Worship

Vital worship occurs where there is effective multifaceted communication of attitudes, values, beliefs, and information:

- Between God and believers.
- Between believers and their fellow believers.
- Between believers and the unchurched.

An exciting by-product of vital worship is evangelism of the unchurched (*see* Psalm 40:3). Biblically, this dynamic is demonstrated in two passages.

The vertical link is communication between God and believers. The impact of this link upon the unchurched can be seen by examining 1 Corinthians 14:24, 25: "But if an unbeliever or someone who does not understand comes in while everybody is prophesying, he will be convinced by all that he is a sinner and will be judged by all, and the secrets of his heart will be laid bare. So he will fall down and worship God, exclaiming, 'God is really among you!' " The vertical component of dynamic worship convinces unbelievers that God is alive and active in the lives of his people. If the vertical component of our worship is dead or stale, it sends a message to the unbeliever: "God is dead—or at least he is not here."

The horizontal component of believers relating to other believers in worship is addressed by Christ in John 13:34, 35: "A new command I give you: Love one another. As I have loved you, so you must love one another. All men will know that you are my disciples if you love one another." Unbelievers will be convinced of the reality of God by the vertical component of our worship of him, and of the fact that we are related to him by the horizontal component.

Vital Worship Is Culturally Relevant

In the last chapter we examined the importance of a culturally relevant philosophy of ministry. One of the prime components of this philosophy is the style of worship employed. When I started CBC I surveyed the community and found that most of the unchurched people I talked to were turned off by hymns. The style of music which they were accustomed to instead could best be exemplified by musical groups such as Peter, Paul, and Mary and the Beatles. So we put our hands on the wealth of worship choruses written during the Jesus Movement of the seventies, and we used synthesizer, electric and acoustic guitars, and drums to accompany the singing.

Had I been planting this church in a remote western town, I may have used bluegrass music, outfitting my worship team with fiddle, banjo and washboard(?). My attire would doubtless have included denim overalls and cowboy boots. The objective, of course, is to determine what is culturally relevant to your target audience and employ it in your worship of God.

Donn Thomas, a church planter who is targeting middle-to-upper-class blacks in upscale Atlanta, has structured his worship service around the culture of his target audience. The black community is by no means monolithic in its worship style but is as diverse as the community itself. Donn's church, Extended Hand Fellowship Church, exudes an intense celebrative worship style that would remind one of their Afro-American heritage. His preaching style is conversational, but highly interactive and responsive.

A multitude of other factors in the worship service also will be culturally related. Building decor will be different for each culture. Stage arrangement, the presence or lack of a podium or lectern, and furniture for sacraments all will depend upon the culture you are seeking to reach. How you dress will be determined culturally; many of my colleagues ministering to contemporary congregations are abandoning clerical robes for shirt and tie, or for three-piece business suits, or sometimes even for shorts and Izod shirts. At our Friday evening worship service during the warmer months in the mild Southern California seasons, the presence of bare legs and thongs on stage is not a rarity.

Worship days and times will be determined culturally. In our particular culture here in Southern California, most unchurched people seemed geared to services presented late Sunday mornings. However, we have two Friday evening services which have been successful as well. Rick Warren has a Saturday evening service targeting professionals who may be working on Sunday morning. (For those who are concerned about keeping the Sabbath, remember that the Sabbath begins on Friday evening and concludes on Saturday evening.) I have yet to see a church whose primary worship service is midweek, but when one comes along I won't be surprised.

The style of teaching also will need to be culturally relevant. Many more churches are discovering that a more relaxed, relational, and frequently more concise sermon, peppered with plenty of unexpected methods of communication, such as audiovisual presentations, drama, interviews, or other devices to keep the message fresh, serves their audience better than the old style of lengthy, pulpit-pounding homiletic monologues.

To this end, pastors should study communication dynamics carefully to help them adapt their presentation to their culture. One of the premier principles of communication most ignored by many preachers is that the unexpected communicates. In one of my more memorable sermons, I just had started to preach on tithing when I was interrupted by an actor planted in the congregation who stood to his feet and loudly began to dispute what I was saying. Another sermon featured an audio voice-over, which had the effect of the cartoonist's thought bubble, in which my prerecorded self was debating whether or not the audience was paying attention to what I was saying.

Tom Nebel is a master at this sort of communication dynamic. He has preached devil's advocate sermons where he took the role opposing the truth he was attempting to communicate. He also does dramatic sermons such as "two truck drivers on the road to Emmaus" who pick up a rather interesting hitchhiker. Another very effective tool is a children's sermon during which he gathers the children of the church around him for a story, with the adults listening in the background.

At CBC we discovered that communication effectiveness increased when we shortened sermons from forty-five minutes to twenty-five minutes. The result was better retention, better energy, and less wear and tear on the preacher!

The level of audience participation will be an important culturally determined factor. It is fascinating to see the dynamic of many Pentecostal or black congregations who give constant feedback to their preachers with shouts of "Amen!" "Preach it!" "Hallelujah!" "Yes, Lord!" and so on. Many times I have wished for a similar device by which to measure whether or not I am getting through to my reserved listeners, most of whom seem to have the expressionless blank mask of someone watching a boring television show!

A final important culturally relevant factor contributing to worship is the layout of the worship location and the amenities provided. You might find a refreshment table to be a welcome addition to your worship service if you are attempting to achieve a more informal atmosphere. If you offer coffee, tea, or soft drinks there might be the added benefit of the stimulant which will help keep your congregation awake during the service! (Don't quote me on that one, please!)

At CBC we have experienced a problem related to our Southern California "hurry" culture: Everyone zooms out the back door as soon as services are finished, rather than staying around and fellowshiping with one another. Some churches are beginning to explore creative solutions to this problem. Tom Nebel's Whitewater Community Church intentionally dismisses its children's Bible classes fifteen minutes later than the adult worship service, forcing the exiting adults to socialize together while they are waiting for their kids to appear.

Vital Worship Is a Team Effort

Cultivating a good worship team is a crucial building block of success in the growing church. Using a team to lead worship shares the responsibility among variously gifted servant leaders and avoids the dangers of making your church a one-man show. It brings balanced perspective and adds creativity to your worship services.

What do you look for in recruiting a worship team? This process has its unique benefits and dangers, given the fact that the up-front aspect of leading worship tends to attract individuals who may be stage or performance oriented—in other words—hams. One of the first qualifications is that all worship-team members be *team players*—not lone stars.

Ray Stedman of Peninsula Bible Church lists four characteristics to focus on when seeking a team player: someone with a searching mind, a humble heart, an evident gift, and a faithful spirit. A critical lack in any of these four areas will cause you headaches to no end.

Obviously, musical ability—particularly a strong sense of rhythm—also will be requisite for someone leading your worship. The leader should have a simple, clear voice which projects well and is easy to follow; an energetic and demonstrative ethos; and a good sense of humor.

However, I have listed these characteristics as secondary to the characteristics of a team player for a good reason. If you are confronted by a choice between a mediocre musician who is a good team player over a good musician who is not, *always* take the former and not the latter. This is one position where, over the long haul, character is far more important than skills. Skills can be developed along the way, but proper character immediately will be necessary for quality worship leading.

A worship team leader must be actively involved in worship planning as well as in worship leading, so this person also must be an able goal setter and evaluator. The leader must be able to get his or her ideas from brainstorm stage to paper to reality. This brings us to our next characteristic of vital worship.

Vital Worship Is Strategic

Like a successful church, successful worship is strategic. That is, every element is well planned in advance by the worship leaders.

First, the worship behavior that the worship leaders desire to occur must be modeled by those who are leading. People will follow the behavior modeled by their leaders. I have visited churches whose song leaders looked as if they had overstarched their underwear and simply were miserable because of it. Guess what? The worshipers all looked the same way. They simply were good followers, taking their cue from their leader.

If you desire your worshipers to move into a high-energy phase of celebration, your worship team must lead them there by prompting the congregation with an even higher exhibit of celebrative energy. If the next phase calls for quiet reflection, worship leaders must be quiet and reflective, setting the pace for the worshipers.

A clear theme and focus is the second most crucial element of a strategically planned worship service. In order to have a theme, you must have a specific response goal by which you can gauge whether or not the worship service has accomplished its purpose. To arrive at such a goal, you, as a pastor, must spend time praying and sensing exactly what God would like to accomplish in the lives of your congregation this week. This goal should be simple—stated in a single sentence— and, like all other goals, achievable, measurable, and challenging.

You'll need to plan worship services well in advance. We began the process at least three months in advance by praying about and outlining our communication goals. We used a worship planning sheet on which we figured all elements of the worship service, including the transitions, even the time *to the minute* required for each element. But many times at the last moment, the Holy Spirit convinced me we needed to change our goal, and we went through the entire process a second time. The result was always that these services accomplished a great work in the hearts of people in our congregation.

This illustrates an important principle, which I call strategic flexibility. Simply stated: Always have a plan—but always be open and willing for God to change it at the last moment to accomplish what he desires.

When planning a worship service in accordance with your stated theme, ask this question about each element: "How will this relate to our theme this week?" If you cannot answer it to your satisfaction, cut or change the activity. Activities which you can link to your theme may include:

- Music (congregational singing, special music)
- Scripture
- Prayer
- Media/drama/puppets
- Announcements
- Offering
- Applause
- Responsive reading
- Communion
- Baptism
- Body life/testimonials
- Parent-child dedication
- Silence

The concept of *focus* is important to understanding how worshipers proceed through a worship service. The clearest analogy once again is an athletic event. In a football game, the focus of the entire stadium is directed clearly upon the pigskin and the person who has it. Many other players are doing many other important things simultaneously, but the goal is to facilitate what is happening with the football at the moment.

So a worship team must consider the dynamics of focus. There must be a specific and clear passing of the baton. Whoever has the baton at the moment is responsible to communicate clearly what is happening, to lead the congregation to your worship goals. Distractions must be minimized so that maximum focus may be applied to whomever has the baton at the moment. Every moment must be accounted for; you want no lapses—no dropped batons—which detract from focus and cause the service to lose momentum.

Many pastors balk at the idea of having a worship rehearsal, but I believe that it's absolutely necessary for quality worship if you have specific worship goals you desire to achieve in your congregation. Dress rehearsals allow you to pinpoint possible hazards in the form of weak transitions or loss of momentum, in addition to giving your worship leaders polish and confidence in what will occur during the service. A preliminary rehearsal should be scheduled with the entire worship team several days in advance of the service, and then the team should meet again at least one-half hour before the service for reorientation and prayer.

A multitude of things can distract from focus. A poor sound system is one of the primary offenders in most churches. Nothing loses a listener more quickly than poor sound quality or too-low volume. Air temperature, quality of seating, and other comfort-related features are other potential distractions. Poor lighting is another offender.

Other distractions can't be foreseen. Wally Hostetter recalls the first time he decided to dispense with a podium and preached holding his Bible in one hand. He asked a woman in the congregation to evaluate and critique the entire service for possible distractions. Afterward he asked her what she thought of the sermon, and she responded, "I didn't hear a word of it."

"Why not?" he asked, surprised.

"You have a marker in your Bible with a little red tassel on the end of it," she told him. "The whole time you were preaching it was swinging back and forth like a hypnotist's pendulum."

This demonstrates the value of planting one or two individuals in each worship service with the capacity to evaluate critically all aspects of the service. They can alert you to distractions and give you feedback on the effectiveness of the various forms of communication used.

A third crucial dynamic of strategic worship is *flow*. Transitions should be smooth and quick, with flow of the worship rapid and dynamic. You have a great deal to accomplish and a short time in which to do so. Your congregation will need to receive from you a sense that you are heading toward a definite conclusion, and that they will need to hang on to their seats on the way there. To have a smooth flow means that not a moment of time will be wasted. To emphasize this, synchronize watches with your worship team and start at the precise minute your service is scheduled to begin. Also work very hard to end at the precise moment the service is scheduled to end. As you are planning your worship service, identify some buffer activities that can be cut (usually later verses of songs) in case you fall behind schedule or in case the Holy Spirit does something you do not expect. Also establish a method of communication with worship-team members that will allow you to acquaint any key players with schedule changes. In CBC's worship services, we even employ occasionally the use of miniature radio headsets to send discreet messages among the key players. It may sound like "Mission Impossible," but it works!

Fourth, a strategically planned worship service *maximizes audience participation*. For every service, consider each element and look for ways that you can bring the congregation into what is happening. Liberal use of humor and occasional lighthearted spontaneous interaction among worship team members or with members of the audience contributes to this end. Responsive readings, interviews with ministry leaders, personal testimonies, a congregational sharing time, body life sharing of Scripture or words of prophecy or knowledge from the Lord, teaching in a question-answer format, and plenty of congregational singing all will be valuable tools.

Finally, Vital Worship Is Multifaceted

Byron Spradlin says:

Worship is more than just music. The entire worship environment is crucial. In fact, we believe that the entire service is the sermon vis-à-vis Marshall McLuhan—and not just the teaching segment of it. We just need to make sure the medium is based on the biblical message, which Jesus himself modeled.

I believe Jesus was the ultimate multimedia presentation of who God is and what he does. What does John say? "In the beginning was the Word, and the Word was with God, and the Word was God . . . . The Word became flesh and lived for a while among us . . . " (John 1:1, 14) In his epistle he adds, "That which was from the beginning, which we have heard, which we have seen with our eyes, which we have looked at and our hands have touched—this we proclaim concerning the Word of life" (1 John 1:1).

The Results of Effective Worship

Here are some goals that you can establish in order to achieve effective congregational worship.

EFFECTIVE WORSHIP WILL BE MEANINGFUL TO REGULAR ATTENDERS. They will leave feeling that their eyes have been lifted from their own problems and onto the Lord. They will be refreshed and revitalized in preparation to face a new week.

EFFECTIVE WORSHIP WILL BE COMPREHENSIBLE TO NEWCOMERS. It will be devoid of Christian jargon that communicates to the unchurched that we are an exclusive club with obscure prerequisites. The unchurched will understand why we meet together, and why we do what we do, and what the perceived results and benefits will be.

EFFECTIVE WORSHIP WILL BE ALIVE TO THE PRESENCE OF GOD. Both regular attenders and newcomers will sense that the whole of what happened was greater than the sum of its parts—that there was an added element that only could have been contributed by the presence of the Spirit of God. As you progress through the service, the fact that God is there moving and working among you will be a foregone conclusion. You will address him conversationally and do all that you do in order to please and honor him.

FINALLY, EFFECTIVE WORSHIP WILL BE RESPONSE ORIENTED. Your focus always should be not on accumulating cognitive knowledge, but on *personal life response.* Here's what the Bible says God is like and here's how he wants us to respond. What are we going to do about it this week?

Objective Measures of Effective Worship

Effective worship will be measured objectively by:

1. THE NUMBER OF PEOPLE ACTIVELY PREPARING FOR IT. How many people serve on your worship team? Do you involve a variety of gifted people for maximum participation and creativity? Does your worship team eagerly anticipate meeting with God? Have you communicated in advance, and have they prayerfully prepared themselves? Are they on time and paying attention to what is happening?

2. WORSHIP ATTENDANCE. Worship attendance is a simple but telling gauge of how well you are succeeding at worshiping God in an effective manner. Study not only your total attendance, but also your attendance patterns. What is the percentage of individuals who faithfully are attending? Are there observable correlations between certain types of activities and attendance? What are the attendance patterns at various services on different days or times? If you don't have an effective system for tracking and analyzing attendance, get one in place. It will be one of the most valuable tools in monitoring your effectiveness in worship.

3. THE NUMBER OF INDIVIDUALS IN YOUR WORSHIP SERVICE WHO ARE PROUD OF WHAT IS HAPPENING AND HAVE SUFFICIENT OWNERSHIP OF IT TO INVITE THEIR RELATIVES, FRIENDS, AND NEIGHBORS. This means you will survey your newcomers to discover why they are there. Pay very close attention to the source ratios. Watch for correlations between changes in your worship services and higher or lower percentages of newcomers invited by regular attenders.

4. FEEDBACK FROM THOSE EXITING THE BACK DOOR. Take your cue from Wally Hostetter, who conducts exit interviews with everyone who fades away. This means, of course, you will be tracking attendance and will need to define what it means to fade away. This may mean someone who misses three out of four consecutive worship services, or four out of five. You can adjust the numbers as you see fit. Pay particular attention to escaping sheep who fall within the target audience defined by your philosophy of ministry. Call them and ask them, "Why are you leaving? What could we have done better to encourage you to stay?"

5. ANNUALLY SURVEY YOUR MEMBERS TO DETERMINE WHAT THEY DO AND DON'T LIKE ABOUT WORSHIP. Take very seriously what you learn from these surveys.

6. LISTEN TO AUDIO OR VIDEO RECORDINGS OF THE ENTIRE WORSHIP SERVICE. Evaluate where the weak points are in terms of distraction, focus, transition, or flow. Note your audience's nonverbal feedback. Note what works and what doesn't, and determine to do more of what works and less of what doesn't!

Action Steps

Cultivate your personal worship. Is it:
  A way of life?
  Regular and periodic?
  At least as vital as what you desire your congregation to experience?
  Free to express before God whatever he puts in your heart to express (no boxes or limitations upon God)?

Clarify your style of worship based on the identification of your target group.

Develop a worship team with these characteristics:
  searching mind
  humble heart
  evident gift
  faithful spirit
  musical ability—sense of rhythm
  clear voice

Involve your worship team in worship planning.

Establish a worship rehearsal.

Continually evaluate your worship effectiveness.
  Plant at least two individuals in the congregation who can help you evaluate.
  Survey your congregation at least once a year.
  Listen to audio and/or videotapes of the service.
  Use a worship evaluation sheet that asks the following questions:
    Is there a clear and unified theme?
    Do all elements of the worship service relate to the theme?
    Are the transitions smooth? Does the service flow well?
    Is the worship God centered and Bible based?
    Is it response oriented? Is there clear application?
    Is the environment positive and conducive to worship?
    Is there a good balance of celebration and reflection?

Was the worship culturally relevant?
Did it relate to the needs of the worship participants?
Was the congregation fully involved in what was happening?
Was the worship fun, enjoyable, enthusiastic, refreshing?
Was it relational?
Were leaders genuine? Did they exude a positive ethos?
Did the service stay to the time schedule? (This question may not be relevant in some cultural settings.)
Try to gauge the feelings of the participants. Did they consider the worship:

Progressive
God oriented
Moving in the right direction
Humorous and fun
Exciting and enthusiastic
Encouraging participation
Open
Relational
Smooth and flowing
Purposeful
Comfortable
Refreshing and freeing
Fast paced
Real or transparent
Celebrative
Reflective
Easy to listen to and comfortable
Proper and Bible based
Encouraging closeness to God

For more worship information, you can contact Artists in Christian Testimony (ACT) at:

ACT
9521 Business Center Drive
Suite A
Cucamonga, CA 91730

Phone: (714) 987-3274.

ACT is a missions organization integrating artistic communications into church and missions ministry.

Principle 5

Holistic Disciple Making

Jesus went through all the towns and villages, teaching in their synagogues, preaching the good news of the kingdom and healing every disease and sickness. When he saw the crowds, he had compassion on them, because they were harassed and helpless, like sheep without a shepherd. Then he said to his disciples, "The harvest is plentiful but the workers are few. Ask the Lord of the harvest, therefore, to send out workers into his harvest field."

Matthew 9:35–38

Through the example of our Lord's life and through his words, Christ gives a dual imperative to his Church. The first is to reach out in love and express compassion for the needs of the whole man. The second, even more specific, is that we are to share the Good News that Christ came to reconcile men to God. Together these imperatives constitute both the means and the essence of the Great Commission—making disciples of all nations.

The Church in the twentieth century has, for the most part, polarized into two factions which argue about which of the two imperatives we ought to obey. The mainline faction argues that the correct imperative is Christ's command and example of caring for the needy and downtrodden. On the other hand, the fundamentalist faction argues that the correct imperative is Christ's command and example of sharing the Gospel message.

Clearly, the time has come for those who believe in following the whole teaching of Christ to frame the question differently. Rather than ask, "Which command ought we to obey?" we should be asking, "How can we begin obeying *all* of Christ's commands?"

The church which seeks to obey the whole teaching of Christ will find that each imperative dovetails with the other. Simply to extend compassion to the hurting with no deeper spiritual agenda is to seek to cure the symptom and not the cause. On the other hand, to preach to the spiritual needs of man's heart without addressing his physical needs as well is to become the hypocrite who turns away his needy neighbor with friendly words: "Go in peace, and be filled!"

Recently, I met Jim DeGolyer of Gospel Outreach. He was among a group of Christians who traveled to Guatemala from Eureka, California, following the disastrous 1976 Guatemala City earthquake. Their intent simply was to express God's care for hurting individuals, in hopes that they also would have opportunity to share the Gospel with those to whom they were ministering. They dug wells, built bridges, and erected hundreds of wooden and block houses.

Soon Jim and his young family discovered that a church was forming around them as they sought to minister. People were drawn to their genuine love and compassion, and as those people became Christ's disciples they drew others in with them. The Christians lived communally, and their evangelism flowed directly from their outreach.

Today, fifteen years later, a Hispanic congregation of 4,000 in Guatemala City thrives. The church has 150 cell groups, four satellite congregations, and has planted a large number of daughter churches throughout Latin America and some in the States. They have begun government-blessed schools and orphanages, Christian communities, and many other ministries among the Latin American poor. They even have a newly established church in Managua. Already it is six times the size of the average church in the United States. Furthermore, they even have sent missionaries to Cuba!

Thousands have been won and many more have been touched by the love of these Christians who were willing simply to obey Christ's dual imperatives and follow his example of compassion.

The Strategic Objective

Being Good News is just as important as *sharing* the Good News. The Bible devotes much more space to demonstrating how Christians should act as redeemed members of the kingdom than to what they should say. John Hayes, vice-president of CRM's InnerChange ministry, warns that Christians cannot separate words from works.

Throughout Scripture, faith is demonstrated and defined not by the words one utters but by the works that one does. James points this out very succinctly.

Religion that God our Father accepts as pure and faultless is this: to look after orphans and widows in their distress and to keep oneself from being polluted by the world.

James 1:27

Later he writes:

As the body without the spirit is dead, so faith without deeds is dead.

James 2:26

The curriculum for making disciples is a multidisciplinary one. First is the influence that we wield as Christians:

You are the salt of the earth. But if the salt loses its saltiness, how can it be made salty again? . . .

Matthew 5:13

Next is our ministry of compassion:

The Spirit of the Lord is on me, because he has anointed me to preach good news to the poor. He has sent me to proclaim freedom for the prisoners and recovery of sight for the blind, to release the oppressed, to proclaim the year of the Lord's favor.

Luke 4:18, 19

I tell you the truth, anyone who has faith in me will do what I have been doing. He will do even greater things than these, because I am going to the Father.

John 14:12

And finally there is the sharing of the message:

Devote yourselves to prayer, being watchful and thankful. And pray for us, too, that God may open a door for our message, so that we may proclaim the mystery of Christ, for which I am in chains. Pray that I may proclaim it clearly, as I should.

Colossians 4:2–4

All three factors—who we are, what we do, and what we say—work together in the process of disciple making. If we are missing any element, our disciple-making efforts will be fruitless.

The Great Commission sets disciple making as our strategic objective. Throughout most of this century the Church has focused its attention on the *sending* imperative—"Go therefore"—rather than on the *making* imperative—"and make disciples." But the focus clearly is on the objective of making disciples—both more and better disciples. This is a very large expectation, but he offers us a great deal of help in this task.

God's Role in Disciple Making

THE ROLE OF THE HOLY SPIRIT.   The Holy Spirit's arrival brought an arsenal of effective disciple-making tools that addressed both the qualitative and quantitative issues. The second chapter of Acts demonstrates this quite well. Until the Holy Spirit came, the disciples waited in the upper room, not impacting the world around them—like many fortress churches today. The day the tongues of flame descended and the Holy Spirit began his work among them their disciple-making ministry exploded. They began to draw a crowd. Obviously the first thing the Holy Spirit did was to move them out of their fortress—and something began to happen:

> Utterly amazed, they [the crowd] asked: "Are not all these men who are speaking Galileans? Then how is it that each of us hears them in his own native language?". . . About three thousand were added to their number that day.
>
> Acts 2:7, 8, 41

The remainder of the second chapter of Acts describes that early group of believers and clearly shows the quality of the Holy Spirit's work. Those thousands in the crowd who responded positively to the message simply didn't go on along their way; instead their lives were radically altered to bring them into conformity with the Church that God desired them to become. The presence of the Holy Spirit and the fact that he was allowed to work unhindered through the lives of the apostles enabled them to reap a bountiful and robust harvest that day.

THE ROLE OF PRAYER.   Christ shows us that the harvest to which we are called is plentiful; in order to reap it we must pray for "workers" (Luke 10:2). God prepares and sends individuals to help us make disciples of the abundant raw material all about us in accordance with our prayers to that end. Sometimes it is necessary for God to prepare us before he can use us effectively.

The Imperative of Compassion

Sci-fi buffs will recall a spine-tingling line from the movie *2010* where Dave Bowman, an astronaut long thought lost, appears on the video screen in his wife's apartment and informs her, in a voice garbled with the static of many light years' transmission distance, that "something is about to happen to the earth." In response to her startled query, "What, Dave? What is going to happen?" he simply says with a knowing smile and the hesitation of someone trying to put something indescribable into words: "Something . . . something wonderful."

During 1988 God did something very unexpected at CBC, and we're still trying to sort out exactly what happened and why. It was, in Bowman's words, "something wonderful." It started as a response to prayer for revival, prayer on the part of several people (like Rose Schuster) for almost ten years. The first symptom was an indefinable difference in the quality of our worship. We became more aware of God's presence, more broken by our fallenness, and more serious about getting down to business with God. As God moved them, people became more open to selfless forms of worship. They experienced a profound repentance and sorrow over sin, a grieving process sometimes lasting for weeks on end.

I was speaking on the subject of revival throughout the world, and even though I felt much opposition in my own spirit, when the time came to communicate God's message I felt that scales were lifted. I saw tears in the people's eyes again and again as the Lord gave me the words to speak. Afterwards, in worship, people fell down on their knees and on their faces before God. We sensed that God was present, moving among us, and that he had pushed us up against the foot of some mountain of greater knowledge of his presence and glory of his working. We found ourselves asking, "What is the next step of faith? Do we have what it takes, as a church, to move that next mountain and see the miracle that God will do among us as a result?" Those were exciting days I never will forget.

After this cycle of repentance and cleansing, something else interesting began to happen. Our church leaders became aware of the church's fortress mentality and our glaring lack of ministry to the needy beyond our walls. Christ's account of the final judgment became a personal challenge to us:

> Then the righteous will answer him, "Lord, when did we see you hungry and feed you, or thirsty and give you something to drink? When did we see you a stranger and invite you in, or needing clothes and clothe you? When did we see you sick or in prison and go to visit you?"
>
> The King will reply, "I tell you the truth, whatever you did for one of the least of these brothers of mine, you did for me."
>
> Matthew 25:37–40

The Holy Spirit began moving people in our church to open up their hearts and reach out to hurting people in our community. The high school kids in our church pooled their money, bought twenty-seven turkeys and fixings, and delivered Thanksgiving dinner to poverty-stricken residents of a mobile home park just twenty minutes away from our church. What they saw caused a surge of compassion—people crammed ten to a trailer, with no furniture, no utilities, very little food and clothing, living in squalid and unsanitary conditions.

Our high school students established a regular ministry of collecting food, clothing, furniture, and toys from people in the church and delivering it to the mobile home park on a monthly basis.

Individuals in our congregation began to respond. They stopped on the streets when they saw homeless people or families, bought them groceries, and then invited them to church. They began visiting local retirement homes. Some helped a local charity prepare meals for the homeless and host dinners in a local park. Several people, including my wife, Janet, began ministering in local prisons and correctional facilities. One man became involved in a support group for AIDS victims.

Cell groups also began to get involved. During the Christmas season almost all of the fifty cell groups in the church were ministering in some way—visiting convalescent homes, participating in Prison Fellowship's Project Angel Tree (buying Christmas gifts for the children of prisoners), taking dinners to poor families, and helping those in need in a variety of ways. We took a special Christmas love offering targeting world disaster relief, church planting, and the needs of the local poor, and raised more than $18,800 (above and beyond regular giving, which includes something for each of these purposes).

CBC is just beginning down this road of kingdom ministry. I look to my brother Frank Tillapaugh and the Bear Valley Baptist Church in Denver, Colorado, as models of what can happen when a church is devoted to Christ's imperative of compassion. Members of Bear Valley are so excited that the pastors "have had to establish very strict criteria governing the start of these ministries," Frank told me. "People have to commit themselves to raising up their own leadership, raising their own support, and so on."

It wasn't always this way in Bear Valley. Ten years ago, when Pastor Tillapaugh began to preach about the importance of reaching out to others, extending a cup of cold water in Jesus' name, not a single person in his church was reaching out in kingdom ministry to the needy of the surrounding communities, and no one seemed interested. As a matter of fact, Tillapaugh reports, it took six years of preaching before the very first outreach ministry was begun.

But today the people of Bear Valley can't seem to get enough of loving others in Jesus' name. Through a coffeehouse, medical clinic, ministry to unwed mothers, and many more outreaches, the members of Frank's church are touching nearly eight thousand needy lives in the Denver area each month.

Most churches have such a variety of needs in their own backyard that they shouldn't have to look very far to find ways that they can minister. When God provides the compassionate leadership, in response to your prayers, you will find the need for ministry to:

- The deaf
- Prisoners
- Orphans
- Widows
- Substance abusers
- Broken families, battered women
- The hungry, homeless, and poor
- Crisis counseling
- Shut-ins and terminally ill
- AIDS victims
- The elderly
- The grieving
- Unequally yoked women
- Child abusers or their victims
- Sexual addictions
- Pregnant teenagers
- Runaways

and the list goes on and on. We are surrounded by opportunities to extend Christ's love. What we need are leaders and workers committed to obeying Christ's imperative of compassion.

Praying for Opportunities

Prayer also helps us to recognize opportunities for disciple making. To some extent disciple makers make their own opportunities, but it's also an issue of recognizing the opportunities already all around us. A thirsty and tired Christ sat down by Jacob's well in Samaria and saw a Samaritan woman who had come to draw water. Few would have recognized this as an opportunity to make spiritual inroads into an entire group of people. Yet Christ saw and seized upon that opportunity (John 4:4–42).

I also have learned by experience that God creates opportunities in answer to our prayers. I cannot remember a time when I have prayed in the morning that God would bring me an opportunity that day to minister in a special way to some person's need and thus draw that person closer to the kingdom, that he did not honor that request.

A mind-set of opportunity focuses on two issues: *existing relationships* and *receptive people*. In our newcomers' class at CBC we helped our people map out their *networks of relationships*, and then consider and pray about which of those unchurched people in their networks God would have them reach out to, and how. Because a large part of the evangelism dynamic is demonstration as well as exhortation—show me as well as tell me—network evangelism is the most effective kind of evangelism. This becomes clear when you see statistics dealing with why people come to our churches. Nearly *nine out of ten come as a direct result of relationships.* As fallible as Christians may be, people still can see God's supernatural love in their lives, and are drawn to Jesus as a result.

Oikos Evangelism

This network evangelism is alternately called friendship evangelism, incarnational evangelism, or *oikos* evangelism. *Oikos* is the Greek word translated "household," and is used frequently throughout the New Testament:

> Then the father realized that this was the exact time at which Jesus had said to him, "Your son will live." So he and all his *household* believed.
>
> John 4:53, *emphasis added*

> He [Peter] will bring you [Cornelius] a message through which you and all your *household* will be saved.
>
> Acts 11:14, *emphasis added*

> When she [Lydia] and the members of her *household* were baptized, she invited us to her home. . . .
>
> Acts 16:15, *emphasis added*

> The jailer called for lights, rushed in and fell trembling before Paul and Silas. He then brought them out and asked, "Men, what must I do to be saved?" They replied, "Believe in the Lord Jesus, and you will be saved—you and your *household.*"
>
> Acts 16:29–31, *emphasis added*

> Crispus, the synagogue ruler, and his entire *household* believed in the Lord. . . .
>
> Acts 18:8, *emphasis added*

These verses demonstrate the fact, widely ignored by our twentieth-century evangelistic methods, that coming to Christ was intended to be a *household* or *network* event. People generally came to Jesus in the context of their group association. As Donald MacGavran has said, if God has indeed prepared the hearts of unchurched people in our community, it is likely he has also built the bridges by which we may reach those people.[1]

If you desire to have a mind-set of opportunity, the second step is to focus on receptive people. Wouldn't it be nice to have a 100 percent positive response to our message? Unfortunately, even Christ experienced a response rate so low that once he even asked his inner core of disciples, "You do not want to leave too, do you?" (John 6:67). No matter how many things we do right, we still will be confronted by unreceptive and unresponsive people.

There is one comforting truth, however: The world is full of receptive people whose hearts God has prepared to receive him. "Do you not say, 'Four months more and then the harvest?' I tell you, open your eyes and look at the fields! They are ripe for harvest" (John 4:35). It's true that some people are planters and some are sowers. I know of missionaries working among Muslim people who probably fall into this category. They are prepared to work years and years planting seeds. It requires a special gift to be a planter or a waterer, because these individuals may be required to invest lifelong labor with no apparent reward.

But for most of us with less patience, we can be grateful to God that he calls us to be reapers. The souls he brings across our paths frequently are hanging like ripe fruit, waiting to be given just the right twist. If we tug and tug again, and they don't come, it may be safe for us to surmise that this particular fruit is not yet fully ripe. A reaper faced with such a circumstance will not brandish his scythe and start slicing away; rather, he simply will find another field that is ready to be harvested.

It is easy to be impatient in the process of discipleship. One of our cell-group leaders, who has the gift of evangelism, invited to his group a pre-Christian man whose personal life crisis had driven him to visit our church. The group meeting came and went with no sign of the man, but two hours later, as the leader was climbing into bed, he heard a knock on the door. He invited the man in. For an hour he listened, and then shared how the emptiness the man was feeling was God's way of nudging him to open up his life to the abundance which Christ desired to pour into him. The man thought a minute, then said, "Let me come to your meeting next week, and perhaps I'll make a decision then."

This leader knows how to give just the right twist, and he hates letting anyone go. Besides he knew he would have a miserable week while praying that the Grim Reaper stayed away from the man's doorstep for seven days. But he knew that this instance required a little patience and a lot of prayer, so he said, "Good. Let's talk next week then," and bid the man good night.

Just as he expected, the week passed very slowly. "I had nightmares of a truck bearing down on the guy just hours before our next meeting," he said. But the fellow showed up in one piece at the next meeting. After the man had talked with the group leader a week earlier, he began wrestling with the claims of Christ. In the privacy of his home, he dismissed his hesitation, got down on his knees, and asked Jesus to come into his heart. "You mean all that worrying was for nothing?" the cell-group leader joked. He had twisted, and while he waited, the ripe fruit dropped into the bag of its own accord!

God gives each of us precisely the same limited amount of our most precious resource—time. Your day has the same number of minutes as there were in the Apostle Paul's. If time were not of the essence, Paul would have been walking his race instead of running it! (1 Corinthians 9:24–27). Our cause will be helped if we focus our efforts on people most receptive to our advances.

Learning to Make Disciples

Individuals must be trained to reach out and make disciples within their networks of relationships. Nothing will happen if you simply sit back and hope.

The first step in training Christians to make disciples is to relieve their unwarranted fears and expectations. Many Christians believe that being involved in evangelism means they will be expected to do door pounding, beach witnessing, street preaching, or engage in some other sales-oriented or high-pressure activity. These activities may be God's assignment for some people, and if so, they will be very fulfilled by doing them. But most of us would rather eat worms. I have vivid memories, as a young college student, of being released into a crowded mall, Bible in hand, to "go witnessing." As I walked along, looking for someone to stop and talk to, my heart pounded and my palms got sweaty. If I could have gotten away with it, I would have ducked behind a large potted plant and hidden there like a fugitive. The fear I felt was so great I barely got even four words out of my mouth, let alone the *Four Spiritual Laws.*

The fact is, I don't think God expects the majority of us to go cold-turkey witnessing. I think he is very happy when we simply focus

on the means he has given us to make an impact in the lives of people
we know and love—and that involves being ourselves, sharing the
Gospel in our own words within our own network of relationships.

So the first step in evangelism training is to eliminate fears that we
will be required to do something unnatural or extremely embarrassing.
At times sharing the Gospel indeed will require that we be like "fools."
But I don't think Paul's intention was that we become brain-fevered,
blithering idiots before total strangers.

You can give people a number of helpful resources to reassure them.
Robert Coleman's *The Master Plan of Evangelism* and Paul Little's *How
to Give Away Your Faith* are two classics. Joseph Aldrich's *Gentle
Persuasion* is very helpful to equip believers without an evangelistic gift.

Make sure people understand, though, that while sharing their faith
should not be a terrifying experience or one that reduces them to
Bible-thumping salvation salesmen, it will be personally challenging.
Sharing an intimate and dynamic faith in an unseen God always will
be a stretching proposition, particularly with those to whom you are
closest. However, God desires us to undertake this challenge in order
that others be presented with the opportunity to respond to his love
and in order that we grow and mature in our own faith.

The next step is to help people identify their networks of relationships. Draw a chart like a wheel and place your member's name at the
hub. Spokes radiating outward will connect with various individuals
in their network of relationships. Prompt them with words like *family,
friends, co-workers, neighbor, postman,* and so on to help them concep-
tualize who the people in their network might be. Then help them
through the process of goal setting. Have them target a specific individual for whom they will pray for opportunities to share Christ. Hold
them accountable for progress in this relationship.

Another important step in the discipleship of your members is to
ensure that they have a solid understanding of the process of evangelism. What is the doctrinal basis for salvation? Key Scriptures? What
is the meaning behind words like *propitiation, redemption, substitution,
atonement,* and *sanctification?* Then make sure that they can share the
essence of the Gospel message *in their own words* by practicing it with
other Christians.

Another valuable part of this process will be helping them to write
out or otherwise present their personal testimony. Effective evangelism usually will be a combination of personal testimony and presentation of the Gospel message. Their testimony should be succinct—one
or two pages at most—and focusing on the positive aspects of how

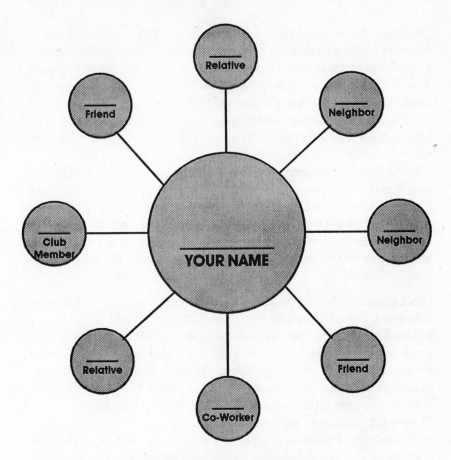

Diagram your networks of relationships

Christ has changed their lives. Then give them opportunity to present it orally to the group, and make sure they receive the feedback and affirmation they deserve for this courageous act.

Peter Wagner teaches that friendship evangelism has three primary facets: *presence, proclamation,* and *persuasion.* In most cases, disciple making will be 80 percent presence, 15 percent proclamation, and only 5 percent persuasion.

PRESENCE. Presence involves building bridges in what we call redemptive relationships. In essence, it's spending time developing trusting friendships with non-Christians. True, friendships are established with a redemptive purpose in mind; but we also must care for the person's needs and respect that person so that we cannot be accused of having a hidden agenda. Relationships are built through pursuing activities of mutual interest. Pre-Christians first must understand that we

Christians are human beings with problems and frustrations just like theirs, but with a God who cares about those problems and desires us to give him our burdens. I don't like the bumper sticker "Christians Aren't Perfect—Just Forgiven" because it sounds like a cop-out for unholy living. Yet this truth assumes greater significance when our pre-Christian neighbors realize that we struggle just as they do, but have a hope and a sincere faith that takes us through with shining colors.

Presence involves actively listening and caring for needs. Deeper still, it means that we will honestly be taking the needs of our pre-Christian friends to God in daily intercessory prayer. If these pre-Christians can see that our God is making a supernatural difference in their lives because we are asking him to, even if they don't believe in him yet, they will not be far from entering the kingdom of God.

PROCLAMATION.   In the best incarnational relationships that I have witnessed, if the Christian is a good enough listener and is expressing the kind of godly compassion that he or she should be expressing, at some point the pre-Christian will invite proclamation. It may be as simple and sincere as the question, "What is it that makes you so different from all my other friends?" or "Why are you doing this for me? Why do you care about me the way you do?" Or it may be less direct. The pre-Christian may ask leading questions to get his Christian friend on the subject of spiritual things. At any rate, the Christian should be praying, watching, and waiting for such opportunities to proclaim the Good News of Christ's death on our behalf and his resurrection to empower us. Like the cell-group leader who agonized for a week over the soul of his searching friend, every true Christian will be painfully aware when a soul hangs in the balance and eager to see a person won over to faith in Christ. The Gospel that we share is, after all, Good News and can be shared positively and with anticipation.

PERSUASION.   Persuasion is simply the twist that causes the ripe fruit to fall into the bag. If fruit truly is ripe, it requires very little twist. King Agrippa said to Paul, "Do you think that in such a short time you can persuade me to be a Christian?" Paul's response is classic, diplomatic persuasion: "Short time or long—I pray God that not only you but all who are listening to me today may become what I am, except for these chains" (Acts 26:28, 29). What a personal testimony! Paul was a persuasive man. He didn't rant and rave, but he reasoned, and he backed up his claims with proof from his own life.

Assimilation and Disciple Making

Throughout much of this century disciple making has been treated as being largely independent of local churches. People were called to Christ in massive tent meetings or crusades which moved into a town or city, had limited contact with local churches, did their business, and then left. With the coming of the electronic media this phenomenon has carried over onto the television screen, with electronic evangelists and the host of problems which accompany that term, wooing people's allegiances (and their dollars), in the privacy of their living rooms, away from the local church.

I believe that disciple making was intended, however, to be a partnership between individual believers and their local church. In addition to the training, encouragement, and support the church could give its members, the church can be the best provider of bridge activities designed to attract and assimilate the unbeliever into the Christian life-style.

Assimilation usually is considered simply in terms of getting the unchurched Christian fully churched. Yet, in a church partnering with its members in order to make more and better disciples, assimilation fulfills a much more significant role.

Most churches, says Wally Hostetter, assume that Christian commitment precedes assimilation. However, in the church that dynamically is reaching out to the unchurched, the opposite may be true. Assimilation into the life of the church may be a valuable tool in bringing the pre-Christian to a point of commitment.

Psychologists tell us that there is truth to the idea that action precedes commitment. The heart follows the will. The biblical ideal of love makes sense because it is an issue of the will. Even if you don't feel as if you can love someone, you let love determine your actions toward them, and the feelings will follow. Involve someone in your church and give him ownership, and his heart will follow. Assimilation precedes commitment.

Hostetter's Faith Church in Detroit encourages newcomers to become involved in church ministries before becoming members. Wally says, "They cannot chair a committee, vote, or be an officer, but they can do almost everything else." As a result, while average worship attendance averages over 500, their membership stands at 249, and each of those members is active in the church's ministry. Coincidentally, last year the church's growth rate was an astounding 45 percent.

Wally was mentored by Bob Davis, who instilled this philosophy of assimilation into him by recognizing ministry potential in the young criminologist and sending him to seminary even before Wally had made a profession of faith in Christ. Davis even paid for Wally's education. "If you graduate from seminary and go into the ministry, consider this a gift," Davis told Wally. "If you don't, consider it a loan."

Rather than being so busy with activities designed to meet the needs of the church's members, a church for the unchurched focuses its energy on events that target the unchurched. Bethany Baptist Church of Long Beach and their felt-needs seminars—potty-training classes for young mothers, financial planning for young couples, and so on—are great examples of this.

These churches make provision for meeting the intellectual needs of seekers. At Willow Creek Community Church in Chicago, this is called the foundations class, which meets weekly and deals with such topics as "Isn't Jesus just one of the ways to God?" At CBC we called this the inquirers' group and followed a small-group format, studying a specific four-week curriculum.

Disciple-making churches gear their worship services to the unchurched. At least once each month the sermon contains a summary of the Gospel message to ensure that newcomers are gaining an accurate understanding of how to commit their lives to Christ's lordship. Social activities at these churches are designed to function as outreach events, and backdoor ministries are implemented to draw in the unchurched through more unconventional means than simply attracting them to the weekend worship services. For instance, the church might host Alcoholics Anonymous meetings, a local scouting troop, music lessons, and so on.

One of the most fascinating sciences arising from within the interdisciplinary church-growth movement is the sociology of how people are assimilated into the mainstream of churches. The Charles E. Fuller Institute has done a tremendous job measuring the factors which assimilate newcomers into a church. This section will provide a summary of some key insights into this process.

The link between disciple making and assimilation is crystal clear. Mature disciples of Christ can be the result only when the new believer or the unchurched person effectively is assimilated into the mainstream of your church, using his gifts and talents to minister to others. An assimilated member embraces the church goals of body life, ministry, outreach and growth, and sharing these goals with the body of Christ is crucial to his spiritual maturity. Likewise, ensuring that the new believer or unchurched person is well assimilated into your church greatly enhances that person's prospects for being equipped to minister and to mature in Christ.

The first step is to define the characteristics of an assimilated person in your church. Here are some key questions you'll want to ask: What is the link between assimilation and membership? Does the person regularly attend worship service? Has the newcomer developed between five and ten new friends within the first six months of attending your church? Does he know what his spiritual gift(s) are, and is he using those gifts in ministry? Is the person part of a cell group or support ministry? Does the person have an identifiable role or task in the church? Does the person give financially? In his speech, does the person refer to the church as "my" church?

Using these questions and others you devise, you should be able to employ a specific instrument that will tell you precisely where on your assimilation continuum each person who attends your church can be found. The following is intended as an example. There is no scientific research to weight the values we have given to various answers, but just a sense of what may be important. You may wish to devise a slightly different scale based on your own research.

Assimilation Continuum

	Score
Member?	
(Yes = +10, No = −10)	_____
Worship service attendance?	
(Regular = +10, Irregular = −10)	_____
How many new friends?	
(0 = −10, +5 points for each, maximum 50 points)	_____
Aware of spiritual gifts?	
(Yes = +5, No = −5)	_____
Using gifts in ministry?	
(Yes = +10, No = −5)	_____
Member of a cell group or support ministry?	
(Yes = +20, No = −5)	_____
Identifiable role or task in the church?	
(Yes = +10, No = −5)	_____

Financial giving?
   (No = −5, sporadically=0, regularly= +5, generously= +10)   _____

Does the person refer to the church as "my" church?
   (Yes = +10, No = −5)   _____

                                                Total Score: _____

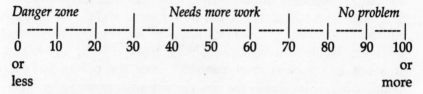

| Danger zone | | | | Needs more work | | | | | No problem | | |

| 0 | 10 | 20 | 30 | 40 | 50 | 60 | 70 | 80 | 90 | 100 |

or   or
less   more

For example: Newcomer Harry is not yet a member, but does attend
worship regularly. He has made five new friends, is aware of his spiritual
gifts, but is not using them in ministry. He is in a cell group, but has no
identifiable role or task in the church. He gives regularly, and in conversation with the pastor refers to the church as "your church." His total
score on this assimilation continuum is forty—partly assimilated, but
teetering on the edge of the danger zone. Get Harry in membership class
and involved in a ministry position using his spiritual gift, and he'll
probably begin referring to "my church" or "our church." You'll have
moved him a long way toward healthy assimilation. Convince him to be
a tither, on top of that, and you'll have it all sewed up.

Essential Elements for Assimilation

What are the characteristics of a church that is assimilating newcomers?

A Healthy Climate

A church with positive communication and a momentum for growth
will exhibit these components of a healthy climate:

LOVE.   Christ said, "All men will know that you are my disciples if you
love one another" (John 13:35). Is there a spirit of loving submission
and acceptance, or are your members criticizing one another, backbit-
ing, rebelling, or complaining?

VISION AND FAITH.   Is your church heading in a specific direction that is
exciting to newcomer and member alike? Do you celebrate the passage
of roadmarks and express your praiseful dependence upon God to take
you to your destination?

SENSE OF SIGNIFICANCE.   Is each person affirmed as a valuable member of the team and made to feel that his or her contribution counts in the scheme of things?

SENSE OF EXPECTANCY.   Is there the recurring notion that something wonderful is about to happen?

A POSITIVE SPIRIT.   Is your communication positive and uplifting, or do you spend all your time pounding the pulpit and criticizing your sheep?

FRIENDLINESS.   Do your people open up to newcomers, greet them during worship services, and invite them to cell-group meetings and church activities?

A Caring Body of Believers

Reaching out to minister to the unchurched is a crucial demonstration of your care for others. Another demonstration is your willingness to offer top-quality services to the newcomers in your church. That means a clean, safe infant nursery staffed by caring people, a quality children's program taught by caring people, a fun and relevant youth ministry led by caring people who can relate to kids and other ministry functions as dictated by the needs of your target audience. It also will mean a friendly, caring pastor who seems both fully human and touched by God in a special way.

Care also will be expressed by having a strategically coordinated method of addressing the emergency needs of those God brings into your path. This will mean a love fund and a proper method of administering it. It also will mean a contact person in the church, or the ability of experienced office staff to make qualified referrals.

An Interesting and Inspiring Worship Service

Your worship should move its participants through the full range of human emotion: laughter, excitement, introspection, and perhaps grief, gratitude, exuberance, and praise. Newcomers must see transparency in worship leaders.

Cultivation of Open Relationships

A diversity of cell groups is the best way to achieve this. Although, as Bill Hybels notes, there must be a certain degree of anonymity as the seeker enters a worship service and begins to check out what this

"Christianity stuff" is all about, on the other hand, there must be plenty of opportunities for developing meaningful relationships where souls can be bared and quality listening can occur. This happens best in cell groups.

People-Flow Analysis

Analyzing people flow means diagramming the path a person takes as he or she moves through your church. He may visit a worship service at the invitation of a friend who is a member. Where will he go from there? What exposure will he receive to other avenues of involvement, and what will be his motivation to pursue them?

The registration slip can be one of the most effective tools for helping to track a person's assimilation path. Beyond being vital for gathering information about first-time visitors, registration slips should be filled out by all who attend a worship service, newcomers and old-timers alike. It should give the worship attender an opportunity to indicate any change which would indicate a transition along that path.

When effectively used with a data-base management system, registration slips will also alert you to attendance problems with a member. Since attendance problems are not only the first signal of a deeper problem, but can also mean illness or other difficulty that you should be made aware of, a well-designed registration slip deserves your full attention.

Many churches assume God will call newcomers to seek involvement, and leave it at that. Sometimes that happens, but most people are bashful enough that they won't get involved unless there is a *hook*—unless someone reaches out and invites them, presents them opportunities to register or somehow begins to depend on their presence, triggers their curiosity, or appeals to their felt needs in some overwhelming manner. What are the opportunities for further involvement at each level? How will people get into a cell group? How will they be attracted to newcomers' class? If they are pre-Christian, how will they be invited to a seekers' or inquirers' group? How will their spiritual needs be evaluated? How will they learn what their spiritual gifts are and learn how to use them? People-flow analysis charts a person's journey through each of these opportunities.

And it doesn't end there. People flow out of a church as well as into it, though hopefully at a slower pace. Pay even closer attention to the path these individuals take. Hold exit interviews with those who have left the back door swinging. At what points could their path of exit have been intercepted?

New-Member Orientation

Early in the life of our church we made a commitment to give a great deal of attention to orienting our newcomers. We devised a seven-week curriculum for this orientation and called the two-hour Sunday-night class newcomers' class. The newcomers' class was intended to help new people:

- Get to know (and be known by) the pastors.
- Get to know other newcomers.
- Receive basic assurance of salvation and beginning discipleship in their Christian life, if needed.
- Learn about how CBC functions: our vision, beliefs, and goals.
- Discover their spiritual gifts and use them in ministry.
- Learn the commitments of membership and have the opportunity to make those commitments.

We started with a schedule of four pastor's classes per year. Beginning in 1980 our church began growing at an explosive rate, and we slowly began to increase the number of these classes, so that by 1985 we were teaching about seven each year.

Such rapid growth has a price. We were stretched thin in terms of facilities and resources, and the growth in our staff had not kept pace. We began to look for luxuries to cut, and one of the things which seemed to be an obvious luxury, because it took so much time and energy, was the newcomers' class. In 1985 we cut back to four.

During 1984 our number of baptisms declined significantly. Because we were used to such rapid growth, this decline came as a great shock, and we were quite perplexed. We spent much time before the Lord, going over all the possible factors and asking, "Why is this happening? What are we doing wrong?"

I remember very vividly that we were at one of our monthly staff brainstorming/prayer retreats. We were crowded into a Jacuzzi, and we were praying and asking the Lord the same questions we had been asking for several months: "What have we been doing differently that might have arrested our growth and caused the current decline?"

It was Rob Acker who got the word from the Lord (if one were less inclined to believe in God's direct communication in prayer, one might say instead, he "came to the realization"). So suddenly he jumped up out of the Jacuzzi, spraying water on the rest of us, and began running around us in circles. He shouted like a man possessed, "Newcomers' class! Newcomers' class! Last year we cut back on newcomers' classes!" At that moment the correlation dawned on all of us. The growth of our church had been linked so closely to the number of newcomers' classes we offered that when, as a result of our exhaustion, we cut back on these, we cut back our growth potential in direct proportion.

So we determined that even if it killed us we were going to upgrade our newcomers' classes and accelerate the schedule. And we did just that. We recruited and trained some quality lay leaders to coordinate the classes, systematized much of the curriculum to put it on automatic pilot as far as the pastors were concerned, and scheduled *nine* classes for 1985. A new class began every five or six weeks, and since they were seven-week classes, there was an overlap, which sometimes meant two nights per week devoted to greeting newcomers and teaching classes.

In some respects the Lord helped take the load, though. A few years later we had begun our network of cell groups, and we realized that one of the things we needed to accomplish in newcomers' class was to give people exposure to and experience in cell-group life. So we split the two-hour class in half, and during one hour we put the newcomers into pilot cell groups. We standardized the curriculum, brought in cell-group leaders and apprentices to lead the groups, and the class practically ran itself during that hour. You can find an outline of CBC's Newcomers' Class in Appendix I.

In 1985 baptisms increased from 45 to 112, and membership addition nearly doubled.

You be the judge as to what extent this sudden growth spurt was a result of our increase in newcomers' classes. But I am convinced that a very direct correlation exists between the energy that you pour into your newcomers—to orient them and assimilate them into the church—and the growth that your church experiences. And for us, newcomers' classes have been the single most effective tool in this process.

Essentials of Discipleship

Effective disciple making addresses the needs of the whole person. It recognizes that it is the Church's primary responsibility to focus attention on these essential components for spiritual health:

DISCERNING GOD'S DIRECTION.   Help people discover God's assignment for their lives, and how they can be equipped to fulfill that assignment.

The greatest satisfaction on earth comes from doing what you know God intended you to do, and doing it well.

SEEKING FIRST THE KINGDOM.   Very few people are beyond the need to be exhorted and held accountable for growth in their devotional life. Are they spending time in the Word daily? Are they praying each day?

CHARACTER GROWTH AND PERSONAL HOLINESS.   Likewise, you must discern and address boldly the issues that keep your people from fellowship with God. Are they experiencing victory over the "sin which so easily besets us"? Are they meditating upon the Word and experiencing that daily confession and renewal so vital to spiritual health?

REDEMPTIVE FAMILY RELATIONSHIPS.   With the breakdown of family values that has occurred in our society in the last fifty years, this is becoming a crucial issue for our churches. Your church will have to deal with divorce, unfaithfulness, single-parent families, broken homes, substance abuse, and other family-related issues just as the rest of society deals with them. How do you exhort your members to follow a biblical model of redemptive family relationships? How can you equip them to stand firm against this erosion of societal values?

VOCATION.   Men long have struggled with vocational issues, and now women have entered the fray. How do we help our members find that vocation God has created them to fulfill? How do we equip our members to be all that God desires them to be in the workplace? How do we help them to understand how they interact with people, and help them to find satisfaction in doing the work to which God has called them?

MINISTRY TO THE BODY OF CHRIST.   People are given gifts by the Holy Spirit solely that they may minister to the body. Discovering how God has gifted you and learning how to use your gift are primary components of spiritual health.

MINISTRY TO THE WORLD.   We come full cycle as we realize that the final step for and proof of those who are discipled fully is their willingness to *empty themselves* in compassionate ministry to those who are near to God's heart—the dispossessed, the poor, the widows, and the oppressed. A growing disciple discerns new ways to disciple people, through body life in cell or small groups, and through one-to-one discipleship—an indispensable tool for establishing new Christians in the faith and developing leaders.

As leaders, we need to realize that our churches are stewards of the resources that God has given us. Those resources are people. To invest those people is to take a risk by expending the energy to evangelize, assimilate, and disciple them. If your church proves itself faithful with its resources—large or small—Christ will add more, and when he comes back from his journey he will say to you, as the master in Matthew 25 said to his servants who had invested their talents: "Well done, good and faithful servant! You have been faithful with a few things; I will put you in charge of many things. Come and share your master's happiness!" (Matthew 25:21).

Action Steps

Keep the vision of making new disciples ever before your congregation.

Provide the permission, freedom, and resources for believers to spend time building relationships. Don't consume their time and energies with purely internal ministries, committees, and church activities. (Most churches can cut their decision-making committees down to one, or two, or three at the most.)

Make heroes out of people who are building redemptive relationships and pioneering dynamic groups. Many churches actually have tried to clamp down on new works that the Holy Spirit was doing as their church members attempted to develop relationships and begin groups to meet felt needs without the official sanction of the church's leaders or committees. Invariably, God removes his blessing from these churches which quench his Spirit.

Establish an assimilation-tracking system that monitors the worship service attendance and follows up newcomers to help incorporate them into the church.

Many fail-safe computer systems will automate the task of tracking based on quantitative data to ensure no one falls through the cracks. At CBC we tracked attendance by hand for many years until a member of our church wrote a computer program, similar to many on the market, which generates letters of concern and raises red flags when certain situations occur—a person starts slipping in worship attendance, stops giving, and so on. These people then can be put on a hot list and contacted by caring members to help determine the nature of the problem and what can be done to correct it. No one ever should be allowed to drift away from your church without notice and concerned contact.

Evaluate your newcomer-orientation process.

Do you have a system (a newcomers' class) easily accessible by newcomers to orient them into your church?

Are newcomers presented and encouraged with regular opportunities to become more involved in your church? What are the *hooks* to motivate them to accept these opportunities?

What training or guidance do you provide to help newcomers? Can they:

Incorporate into a meaningful group?

Become involved in a meaningful role or task?

Understand the commitments of membership, including the importance of regular attendance, cell-group involvement, ministry involvement, and biblical stewardship?

Survey your people and leaders to help discover what your training agenda for next year should include:

Personal evangelism?

Cultivating a deeper relationship with God?

How to become a prayer partner?

How to deal with the issues of divorce, broken homes, single-parent families, and so on?

Counseling and referral networks?

How to be most effective in your ministry?

Marriage and family relationships?

Money management?

Notes

1. Robert E. Logan and Jeff Rast, *Starting a Church That Keeps on Growing* (Pasadena, Calif.: Charles E. Fuller Institute, 1986), p. 18.

Principle 6

Expanding Network of Cell Groups

And let us consider how we may spur one another on toward love and good deeds. Let us not give up meeting together, as some are in the habit of doing, but let us encourage one another—and all the more as you see the Day approaching.

Hebrews 10:24, 25

One of the most influential books I have read in the last year, I humbly will confess, is not one that you'll find on the shelves of your local Christian bookstore. It is called *Thriving on Chaos*, and it is the visionary work of Tom Peters, the same man who turned the world of business management on its ear a decade ago with the appearance of *In Search of Excellence*.

In *Thriving on Chaos* Peters summarizes the findings of a tremendous amount of research with the words:

Take all the evidence together, and a clear picture of the successful firm in the 1990s and beyond emerges. It will be:

- flatter (have fewer layers of organizational structure)
- populated by more autonomous units (have few central-staff second-guessers, more local authority to introduce and price products)
- oriented toward differentiation, producing high value-added goods and services, creating niche markets
- quality conscious
- service conscious
- more responsive
- much faster at innovation
- a user of highly trained, flexible people as the principal means of adding value[1]

When I first read Peters's words I pondered exactly how churches could achieve these ends. I began to gain an insight into this question from several other key passages in his book. Peters augmented his description of the successful firm in the 1990s by saying that it will:

118

- Radically emphasize "specialist" rather than "mass"/"volume" thinking throughout its entire portfolio—now.
- Constantly create new market niches via new products and continuous transformation for every product.
- Continually add more and more values (features, quality, service) to every product or service, youthful or mature, to achieve or maintain true differentiation.[2]

Centralized Versus Decentralized Ministry

What Peters is saying is that the successful organization will shift from a centralized approach in achieving its objectives to a decentralized approach.

Most churches today are centralized rather than decentralized. They are run by a centralized bureaucracy or clergy which operates the programs. The entire organization is dependent upon the flow of ministry through each organizational unit. Though each may be able to focus energy well (one church may sport great Bible preaching, another be known for its warm and caring fellowship, another be a great missionary church) it often will have a low organizational endurance for chaos or change. The church is dependent on narrow organizational functions for survival.

An outstanding example of a decentralized church is well known to most pastors—Dr. Paul Yonggi Cho's Yoido Full Gospel Church in Seoul, South Korea. This church—more than *five thousand times larger* than the average American church— is, in reality, a closely knit network of decentralized home cell groups. Cho describes his church, which at well more than a half million members stands as the largest church in the world, as: ". . . the smallest church in the world as well as the biggest . . . because every member is part of a home cell group consisting of 15 families or fewer."[3]

From the standpoint of this South Korean pastor there are distinct advantages to having ministry in this church decentralized and distributed among his tens of thousands of lay pastors. All churches in South Korea live under the threat of imminent invasion from Communist North Korea. An effective strategy for strangling the typical church would be to remove its pastor, around whom the bulk of ministry revolves. However, removing the senior pastor of a church like Full Gospel, where ministry occurs at the level of the cell group, would do little to stop or even slow the work the Lord is doing among the cell groups in Seoul. Even if the church's buildings were burned down, its assets seized, and its pastoral staff executed or imprisoned, ministry would continue virtually unimpeded at the cell-group level.

And what ministry it is! Every one of the half million members of the church interacts each week in a cell-group body life. Whereas the typical church grows to a point where it stretches to the limit its pastors' ability to minister to each member, a cell-group church has no limit as long as you are effectively mobilizing laity to minister through cell groups.

Though Full Gospel Church is the world's largest, it is by no means alone in its discovery of church growth through cell groups. Ralph Neighbour, professor of church planting at Columbia Biblical Seminary and president of Touch Outreach Ministries in Houston, Texas, told me: "In the last five years, we have seen an explosion of what I call *pure* cell-group models. A cell-group church is actually more of a movement than a local organization. All the cell groups are linked together and compose a larger congregation."

Ralph then proceeded to cite one example after another of churches throughout the world which are expanding rapidly as a result of cell-group growth. Dion Roberts, the pastor of Eglise Protestante Baptiste Oeuvres et Mission in Abidjan, on Africa's Ivory Coast, began to build cell groups in 1985 with a church of 350. In 1989 his church has reported 82,000 people attended their Easter Harvest meeting where 15,000 were converted to Christ. Lawrence Khong's Faith Community Baptist Church in Singapore has more than 3,000 people as of February 1989, and projects growth to 4,000 people by July 1989. Dr. Roger Forster of Icthus Fellowship in London, which is checkerboarding the city with its cell groups, *quintupled* its number of groups in about a year. They keep about twenty members in full-time year-long training at all times to pastor the new congregations spun off to accommodate these cell groups. And in Paris, traditionally known as a very difficult city for ministry, one cell-group church is operating one thousand cells.

Currently, the largest cell-group churches in the United States— New Hope of Portland, Oregon, and Church on the Way of Houston, Texas—are far smaller. A significant cell-group movement also is occurring among the multitude of Vineyard churches, catalyzed by John Wimber in Anaheim, California. But the good news, says Neighbour, is that the cell-group movement in this country is in the preliminary stages of a revolution that soon will sweep us into this whirlwind of growth already occurring worldwide. Neighbor says, "We probably are servicing more than 100 of these new cell-group churches, each having fewer than 150 members. They are brand new, nearly all started by baby-boomer pastors, seminary graduates who served their time in the prison of the traditional church but got fed up. They now are pulling away and starting pure cell-group churches."

Our experience at CBC, small as it is compared to the examples cited above, bears out the potential of the cell-group church. For nine years we worked hard to see our small groups increase from a handful to level off at about twenty. It was only little over a year ago when we made the break from a traditional home Bible study or small-group program. During this first year, which is supposed to be the most difficult for cell-group growth, we have seen a more than 100 percent increase in the number of groups, from an initial twenty-five groups to more than fifty. Taking its cue from this doubling, CBC set its growth goal for its second year of cell groups at one hundred groups. At the rate they are now growing, it looks as though they may enter 1990 having surpassed this goal.

One of the first cell groups to start in our church began with ten members. In five months they had added only one person. They began to make some modifications based on principles discussed later in this chapter, and by the end of the year they had spun off four new groups, with approximately one hundred people participating in all.

Cell groups distribute ministry among the laity and bring exponential growth to their churches. Carl George likens the dynamic of a cell-group church to a field full of mice, growing and reproducing. These mice, or cell groups, also gather for weekly mouse conventions called worship services. The field full of mice is virtually indestructible. However, if you want to cultivate a thriving cell-group ministry in your church, it must be carefully planned and executed.

The Biblical Basis for Cell Groups

Scripture says little about church organization. The first church, with its rampant growth, seemed to have been structured along the familiar lines of the synagogue. As churches grew they shifted from house churches to more centralized entities identified with cities or geographic territories. Though we may know little about their precise structure, we have a great deal more information about their function.

It is important, then, to look at the biblical *function* of the church first, and ask the question, "What structure is most conducive to helping the church fulfill its biblical function?" If examined in this light, it is difficult to arrive at any answer other than "the cell-group church."

These passages reveal a great deal about the biblical function of a healthy church:

Acts 2:42–47. "They devoted themselves to the apostles' teaching and to the fellowship, to the breaking of bread and to prayer. Everyone was filled with awe, and many wonders and miraculous signs were done by the apostles. All the believers were together and had everything in common. Selling their possessions and goods, they gave to anyone as he had need. Every day they continued to meet together in the temple courts. They broke bread in their homes and ate together with glad and sincere hearts, praising God and enjoying the favor of all the people. And the Lord added to their number daily those who were being saved."

Functions: Teaching, fellowship, communion, prayer, miracles, commonality, pooled resources, meeting needs, spending time together, praise, evangelism, assimilation.

Romans 12:10. "Be devoted to one another in brotherly love. Honor one another above yourselves."

Functions: Commitment to fellow Christians, affirming and caring for them.

Ephesians 4:2, 32. "Be completely humble and gentle; be patient, bearing with one another in love. . . . Be kind and compassionate to one another, forgiving each other, just as in Christ God forgave you."

Functions: Being transparent, opportunity to exercise patience and bear with others in love, exercising kindness and compassion, forgiving others.

Galatians 6:2. "Carry each other's burdens, and in this way you will fulfill the law of Christ."

Functions: Listening to and sharing the problems of one another.

Ephesians 5:21. "Submit to one another out of reverence for Christ."

Functions: Mutual submission to others' care.

Colossians 3:16. "Let the word of Christ dwell in you richly as you teach and admonish one another with all wisdom, and as you sing psalms, hymns and spiritual songs with gratitude in your hearts to God."

Functions: Teaching, admonishing, personal life application, praising God together.

1 Thessalonians 5:11. "Therefore encourage one another and build each other up, just as in fact you are doing."

Functions: Encouragement, edification.

HEBREWS 10:24, 25.   "And let us consider how we may spur one another on toward love and good deeds. Let us not give up meeting together, as some are in the habit of doing, but let us encourage one another—and all the more as you see the Day approaching."

Functions: Exhortation, personal life application, meeting together, instilling hope.

JAMES 5:16.   "Therefore confess your sins to each other and pray for each other so that you may be healed. The prayer of a righteous man is powerful and effective."

Functions: Confession, prayer, healing.

As you scan the above list, how many of these functions are fulfilled best by the traditional church structure: large-group worship, possibly combined with mid-sized Sunday-school classes using a predominately lecture format? How many are fulfilled best in cell-group interaction of ten believers who are exercising their spiritual gifts through committing themselves to, sharing with, and caring for one another? In fact, each of these functions can be fulfilled very effectively in a cell-group setting. The medium- or large-group setting, either worship or Sunday school, is much less effective in fulfilling the "one another" functions of the New Testament.

What is the span of care that one Spirit-filled human being can give to others? Christ himself drew the line at 12. Yet here we are, pastors and lay leaders, attempting to draw into our fold and then single-handedly care for the needs of people in groups of 50, 100, 250, 500 and sometimes 1,000 people! Are we greater than our Master?

Although somewhat culture dependent, the number ten seems a mid-range ideal for the amount of people who adequately can be cared for by a Spirit-filled Christian lay minister. At CBC we have found cell groups function best when comprised of between four to twelve people.

The beauty of the cell-group system is that no one, even in a church as large as Full Gospel, ever will have to care for more than that handful of people. Even in the largest cell-group church, the senior pastor interacts directly only with a handful of leaders, who in turn may interact each with another handful, who in turn each interact with a handful, and so on down the line as far as necessary until you reach the level of the cell-group leader and his or her handful of cell-group members.

If you mapped this in the form of an organizational chart, it would look very much like the classic tree with its system of branches. At CBC, we turned this chart upside down, with the care-group leaders on top and the senior pastor on bottom, to illustrate the importance of the care-group leader and the fact that any additional layers of leadership simply exist to serve and facilitate the care groups which are the heartbeat of our church.

I am convinced that one of the key reasons traditional churches have been so ineffective at stopping the moral and spiritual decline of this society isn't humanism, evolution, *Roe* v. *Wade*, the banning of school prayer, or the cults. These are merely symptoms of the disease. The real reason is that we have had almost nothing to offer our unchurched neighbors that effectively fulfills the human spirit's dynamic needs as outlined in the New Testament. These needs clearly were fulfilled by the New Testament church. If we were satisfying the biblical function of the Church, the moral battles in our culture would have been won long ago.

Our generation can begin to fulfill that function—and cell groups will give us the time, place, and reason to do it.

Components of Effective Cells

I wish that we had an entire book in which to discuss this subject. Here is where the rubber meets the road. How do you structure a network of cell groups that successfully will fulfill the biblical functions of the New Testament church?

The Microcosmic Nature of Cells

The foundational cell-group principle is that cell groups should be in microcosm what the Church should be in macrocosm. The greatest hindrance to cell-group effectiveness is not taking them seriously enough and not encouraging them to take themselves seriously enough.

Cell groups are not merely home Bible studies, small groups, discussion groups, or prayer groups. All these titles reflect but one aspect of what a healthy cell group should incorporate. Healthy cell groups must fulfill at least seven key functions found in the portion we read earlier in Acts 2:42–47:

- *Teaching:* Learning *and applying* God's Word.
- *Fellowship:* Building supportive, mutually accountable relationships.
- *Worship:* Praising God for who he is and what he has done.

- *Prayer:* Listening to and sharing intimately with God; interceding on behalf of others and God's work in the world.
- *Power:* Experiencing the filling and outpouring of the Holy Spirit.
- *Ministry:* Using spiritual gifts and loving each other in practical ways to meet needs.
- *Evangelism:* Impacting our society and sharing the Good News so that people become Christ's disciples.

The name by which you address your cell groups should reflect the more serious nature of what you are attempting to accomplish through the cell-group structure. At CBC we call our cell groups care groups. At New Hope they are TLC groups and at Vineyard churches, kinship groups. In the Catholic renewal movement they are called basic Christian communities, and in France, Christ groups. Ralph Neighbour calls them shepherd groups. Most of the cell-group names I've heard reflect their prime function of allowing a small group of believers to exercise intensive biblical love, care, and compassion upon one another.

The Diversity of Cells

Earlier I stated that the cell group should be the Church in microcosm. Churches today—particularly in many world-class cities that are a melting pot of various cultures—are diverse; the way churches worship and minister depends upon the culture or subculture they are targeting. As Rick Warren says, "It takes all kinds of churches to reach all kinds of people."

Thus we can conclude that it takes different kinds of cell groups to minister to different kinds of people. As a church grows it encounters an ever-broader spectrum of needs. When CBC had only 100 people, our needs were relatively simple. We ministered primarily to young and growing families. We needed to form meaningful friendships and to find a way to relate to one another in spite of busy schedules. We needed help raising our young children and advice about our finances.

Now that CBC is attended by almost 1,500 people, our needs are much more diverse. We have many different flavors of singles, from the college-age single, to the young career single, to the divorced single, the single parent, or even the elderly widow or widower. Each has his or her own specific needs. We have children and young people of all ages. We have families at all points on the spectrum. We have the pre-nest family (no kids yet) and the empty-nest family (kids grown and no longer living at home)—and everything in between. We have "unequally yoked" women, adult children of alcoholics, stressed-out executives, those who have suffered in incestuous relationships, and children from broken homes. We have the physically and mentally handicapped. We have all kinds of people, each of whom will fit very well into a cell group—if the people in that group have essentially the same needs and problems and are at approximately the same life stage.

Therefore, the growing church must build an ever-broadening array of cell groups with different focuses, different target groups, and different operating strategies. They may have vastly different forms, but the goal for all of them is to fulfill the same critical cell-group functions.

This equation has another variable. In chapter 2 we spoke about the biblical purpose of leadership: to equip God's people for works of service. We explored the root word translated "equip," which means more literally "to mend" as to set a broken bone or to mend a torn net.

Humanity's fallenness and the path of return to God which Christ has provided has created a *mending continuum* with different people at different points along that torn net. For many, the net is ripped asunder; these have yet to express their faith in Christ as Savior. To help an unbeliever express his or her faith in Christ is to enter the first few stitches in that torn net, starting at the very end of the tear. As the believer yields further to the lordship of Christ, a few more stitches are added. The process of maturing as a Christian adds more stitches until, at some point at or very near glory, the net is mended entirely and the person becomes like Christ in practice as well as in position.

Ministry could be defined as that process of taking people from where they are to where they need to be in Christ. We can't minister to people unless we can determine their point of need—their location on the mending continuum—and what type of equipping is required to move them to where they need to be.

Different types of cell groups are equipped, by virtue of their cellular assignment from God, to pick up people at various points on that continuum. Some groups are designed to put in those first few stitches. Others might pick up young Christians and seek to mature them. Still others will exist to equip mature Christians more fully for intensive ministry, and thus will design their strategy to deal with nets that are mostly whole.

Each group's starting point on the mending continuum may be slightly different. Some groups are led by evangelists, as in a summer moms group led by a woman in our church who saw a need among her neighbors to involve their kids in positive, fun activities during those long summer days away from school. She combines a craft activity for moms and kids with a time of fellowship and inspirational, evangelistic teaching during which child care is provided and moms can flee their little monsters for an entire, wonderful hour.

Other leaders specialize in retrieving lost sheep. One group at CBC was dealing with a couple experiencing difficulty in their marriage. At one point the man fled to Las Vegas, where he planned to engage in activities designed to wreak revenge on his wife for the frustration he was experiencing in their marriage. His care-group leader "just happened" to be traveling to Las Vegas on business, tracked the wayward sheep down, knocked on his hotel door, and put him on a bus headed for home.

Some cell-group leaders have a high level of innovation. Depending on their working style, most leaders simply will desire to be shown how to accomplish the church's goals and then will work faithfully to this end. Other leaders with different working styles will want to forge new paths, "going where no man has gone before."

One leader, facing rapid growth, moved his group from homes into larger church facilities where they began what in essence was a congregation of cell-group clusters, replete with a worship team, child-care workers, fund-raising activities, and so on. The experiment didn't work and his group eventually returned to meeting in homes and multiplied leaders the way a group should. Through innovation we have discovered many of the new paths the Lord has for us, so we never discourage innovation as long as the leaders' hearts are right and they remain teachable and willing to admit failure. It was, after all, through God's innovation—the coming of God's Son in human form to a manger, an innovation so unexpected by the religious leaders of the day that they never did accept it—that we were reconciled to God. God always works in unexpected ways, and if you put him (or other people) in a box you might miss out on his blessing.

Different Kinds of Groups for Different Kinds of People

Multiplying diverse care groups is crucial to meeting more effectively the needs of those God brings into your fellowship.

NUMBER OF GROUPS NEEDED. Sociological studies show that, in order to grow, the average traditional church requires a minimum of six groups for every one hundred people in the church. One way to gauge your church's health and growth potential is to count the number of healthy groups and divide it into your total attendance:

- *Eight or more per hundred: you're in great shape!*
- *Six or seven per hundred: build on this base.*
- *Four or five per hundred: needs some work.*
- *Three or fewer per hundred: Pack your bags!*

The ideal, of course, is that *everyone* in your church be involved in a cell group of ten people. This will be a challenging goal for most churches with home Bible-study programs, which usually have less than 25 percent of their attendance involved.

On the biological level, cells, like mice in the field, are nearly imperceptible units of operation to the casual outside observer who will see the cell's overall effect, the unity of purpose, and the movement toward the kingdom of God. If you have a microscope, however, individual cells are very diverse entities. The human body alone contains thousands of different types and configurations of cells performing many diverse—but all equally valuable functions.

GEOGRAPHIC VERSUS HOMOGENEOUS. In highly mobile cultures whose people would rather drive two miles than walk two blocks, cell groups allowed to form naturally will form on the basis of affinities—people congregating together with other people similar to them. In less mobile cultures, however, the geographically defined cell group may be more common. Although American cell groups may be more effectively structured along lines of shared affinities than by geography, there's always an exception. Ralph Neighbour experienced great success with geographically defined neighborhood evangelism groups at the church he pastored in Texas, which grew from several hundred to more than twelve hundred members in just three years. But these groups still were built along relational lines.

The Leadership of Cells

To be effective, cell-group leaders must be as committed to their cells as effective pastors are to their churches. (Remember—the cell group is the church in microcosm!) Many cell-group churches choose to reinforce this reality by calling their cell-group leaders lay pastors, cell pastors, or a similar title.

Cell-group leaders should be given as many pastoral ministry responsibilities as your theology allows—the more the better. Among our church's most powerful baptism services were those in which a cell-group leader whose group had led a person to faith in Christ also had the privilege of leading that person down into the baptismal waters. I recall the baptism of one fellow who had been a high priest in the Mormon church. He visited our church with his wife, but was on the verge of returning to his Mormon compatriots, whom he had abandoned when the Holy Spirit began making him extremely uncomfortable with the falsehood they were asking him to teach. One of our care groups zeroed in on him and began a weekly regimen of fervent prayer and fasting on his behalf. Several months later, when the group leader challenged him to renounce his priesthood vows and be baptized, he yielded and committed his life to Christ.

I listened as this group leader led this former high priest in a very powerful renunciation of his cultic vows and a commitment to the "priesthood of believers" as he was baptized in a neighbor's pool with friends, family members, and care-group members watching. There was no shortage of tears and hugs as this group together celebrated the miracle of second birth. I reflected that only a healthy cell group could have made such a scene possible.

It is crucial to help cell-group leaders realize the gravity of their assignment. Our cell-group leaders sign a position description explaining the leader's responsibility. Before he or she publicly is commissioned, he should sign such a position description or agreement in a step of personal commitment to carry out his responsibilities of the important office of lay pastor. In Appendix III you'll find CBC's Position Description Sheet for cell-group leaders.

The Four-Fold Leadership Function of Cells

Because cells are a microcosm of church life, body-life dynamics crucial to healthy churches functioning effectively also are important for healthy cells. As with churches, leadership of these cells should be strategic in the sense that the functions must be built in before the cell ever opens its doors to its members.

These functions will be distributed among the cell's leadership team in accordance with working style, gifting, or inclination.

LEADER. This person will have overall catalytic responsibility for ensuring the cell group's health and growth. He or she will be involved in planning, delegating, and leading the leadership team of the cell group.

SHEPHERD. This person is responsible to ensure that every person in the group receives the hands-on care that the group is responsible to give him. He or she should be praying for each member daily and be in contact with each during the week, outside the context of the group meeting.

EVANGELIST.   This person is involved most actively in the growth of the group, bringing in the unchurched or facilitating group members in identifying their networks of relationships and inviting their friends, relatives, and neighbors to attend the group meetings.

HOST.   This person is responsible for ensuring that an environment is established in which the necessary care-group dynamics can occur. Generally a cell group meets in the host's home, and the host arranges or oversees the arranging of refreshments. He or she also may be responsible for planning social or recreational activities for the group.

Many group members excessively emphasize what they perceive as the function of teacher, Bible-study leader, or facilitator over the above functions. However, this falls more into the realm of activity than function and could be accomplished by any group member gifted in teaching or moderating a group Bible or topical study. Many groups, as well, will de-emphasize the Bible study in favor of some other activity, such as a ministry focus or prayer.

This overemphasis on the teaching component of a cell group is what Ralph Neighbour refers to as the cognitive curse:

> We can't get away from our cognitive curse! We have become so used to having an agenda when we meet that church groups often boldly move into home cell groups, only to smother the relational life with more Bible study, more listening to tapes, etc. It almost seems we are afraid to assemble without an agenda!

> The Bride of Christ needs time to reproduce the Upper Room experience, when 120 gathered for 10 days and ended up becoming one! Their unity witnessed so powerfully to the watching unbelievers that 3,000 were added to their number.[4]

From your very first cell group, drill into your leaders the importance of facilitating a balanced body life in which the cognitive component of teaching is only one aspect, on an equal par with other components such as worship, prayer, fellowship, confession, admonishment, prayer, healing, bearing and sharing burdens, and simply spending time together.

Several published resources can assist your leaders in setting an agenda for effective cell-group meetings. Among the most popular are Lyman Coleman's highly relational *Serendipity* Bible study/discussion materials. But other outstanding resources I recently have discovered include materials published by Ralph Neighbour's Touch Outreach Ministries, namely, *The Shepherd's Guidebook, Life Basic Training: A Bib-*

lical Examination of Value Systems, and *Touch Outreach Ministries Basic Training Manual.*[5]

The Importance of Apprenticeship

Paul's relationship with Timothy provides an outstanding scriptural model for the process that must occur in churches if new cell-group leaders are to be equipped. Paul's letters to Timothy reveal a great deal about the mentor-apprentice relationship. "You then, my son, be strong in the grace that is in Christ Jesus. And the things you heard me say in the presence of many witnesses entrust to reliable men who will also be qualified to teach others" (2 Timothy 2:1, 2).

Just as in Moses' day mentors handed down oral traditions and teachings of their fathers, so we as leaders are to entrust the teachings of Christ to those who are *reliable* and *will be qualified* (future tense!) *to teach others.* We are to focus our energies on those willing and able to identify, recruit, and train their own apprentices. If those we seek to equip do not have this goal in their hearts, they are unworthy of our equipping efforts.

Few leaders have the correct perspective of how great an amount of energy and attention must be focused upon the issue of equipping apprentice leaders. During CBC's first year of cell groups we proceeded about this very haphazardly. Occasionally we spoke on the importance of finding an apprentice a leader could train so that his group eventually could multiply. But we didn't establish this as a crucial element which must be in place in order for a group to meet its strategic growth goals.

We now are reorienting our leaders to recognize the importance of having an apprentice in place when the group begins. If they do not have apprentices yet, they are asked during every leadership support meeting, "Have you found the apprentice that the Lord has for your group yet? If not, why not? Are you making it a matter of prayer and fasting?" If they are not, we admonish them kindly but firmly that Christ instructed us not to pray for the harvest, which is plentiful, but for workers to be sent into the harvest.

Our leaders have proven that, if the focus is correct, apprentice leaders can be equipped at a very rapid rate. Personality doesn't have as much bearing as one might think. One woman at CBC, quiet and somewhat shy but with a great heart for raising up leaders, in the first year of her group personally discipled three Timothys who now successfully are leading their own groups and discipling their own Timothys. A male care-group leader who is more outgoing and more outspoken has raised up four leaders in a year. Although the goal we have placed before our leaders is to fully disciple one apprentice in one year, many leaders surpass that goal.

Beyond profession of faith and church membership, CBC has only three absolute requirements for cell-group leaders:

1. They humbly must recognize their need for training and support and therefore attend regularly our leadership support meeting every two weeks.
2. They must submit to the spiritual authority of those who are appointed their leaders and complete a monthly form reporting on their groups, who was in them, and the type and amount of care they received.
3. They must consider it their first responsibility to have an apprentice leader in place when the group begins; if this cannot be done, they must be praying and fasting for such a leader in accordance with the promises of Scripture.

Of course we give a great deal more guidance and ask cell-group leaders to fulfill many more functions. But these are the rock-bottom requirements that embody our leaders' submission to the Lord's authority over their cell groups. Placing priority on the task of finding an apprentice leader is foremost among these three.

Cell-Group Leader Aptitudes

The accomplished cell-group leader will exhibit a balance of three leadership aptitudes: character, experience, and skills.

Of these three aptitudes, only the first is required for entrance into the position of apprentice leader. The apprentice leader must exhibit these godly character qualities:

1. A passion and heart for ministry to the hurting, to the unchurched believer, to the churched but unassimilated believer, or to the unchurched unbeliever.
2. Growing in Christian character, as listed in the qualifications for overseers and deacons listed in 1 Timothy 3.
3. Willingness to submit to spiritual authority, to humble himself, and to jump the hoops of the cell-group leader training and support path.

Committed members of the church who exhibit the desire and these character qualities will be considered for apprentice leaders, regardless of their level of experience or skills. It is expected that the apprentice will gain experience and skills in the process of leading a cell group, first under the tutelage of a cell-group leader, and then as the apprentice himself becomes a cell-group leader.

A Supervisory Structure for Cell Groups

When we first decided to become a cell-group church, although we sought the wisdom of those who were experiencing to some degree what we hoped to accomplish, much of what we had to do was pioneering work. A good example of this is with the supervisory structure for cell groups. We knew that if cell groups were to grow explosively in our church, we would need a supervisory structure that would take the burden of supervision from the hands of the elite professional clergy and put it where ministry belongs—in the hands of the laity. We began searching Scripture for a model.

We stumbled upon Exodus 18. When we read the story of how Moses' father-in-law helped him establish a judicial structure over the children of Israel, we realized the Lord was speaking directly to our church and giving us the key to effective cell-group supervision. We call it the Jethro Principle.

The story's parallels to our church's situation were uncanny. Moses, the "senior pastor" of the children of Israel, saw the Spirit of God move and a great work occur among the 2 million or so Israelites. Like Dr. Cho in the early days of his burgeoning church, Moses and his ambitious intention to sit in sole judgment upon the Israelites, entirely alone, hearing each case requiring arbitration or settlement, put him in grave

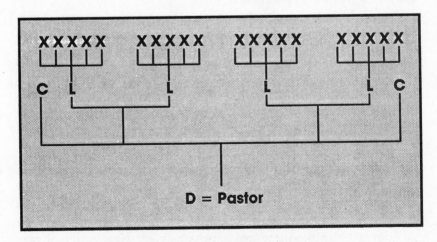

Modified Jethro Supervisory Structure for 200 Adults

danger of that classic senior pastor's disease—burnout. Fortunately Jethro gave him the right counsel at just the right time.

Jethro suggested a structure whereby each of those 2 million Israelites was clustered into a group of 10 (sound familiar?), with a leader placed over it. Next came leaders of 50, each relating to 5 leaders of 10. Next were leaders of 100, then leaders of 1,000. These were the people Moses counseled. Moses still was relating to a large number of people—approximately 2,000—but he was an extraordinary man, and doubtless this was a simpler task than what he originally had attempted.

In the illustration on page 133, Roman numerals are used to illustrate the various positions of the Jethro system. Carl George helped us modify Jethro's judicial system for application to our church's discipling context. We have become accustomed to Carl's terminology embracing these representations:

X—A shepherd of ten, or cell-group leader (also called lay pastor)
L—A leader of fifty, or cell-group coordinator, who coaches five X's.
C—A gatherer of mid-sized groups (forty to one hundred people) in order to help form new cell groups.
D—A leader of five hundred overseeing ten L's and five C's. This ordinarily is filled by a full-time staff member or pastor.

Because each of the four positions is responsible for developing an apprentice, we also have an additional set denoted as Xa, La, Ca, and Da for each of the apprentices.

The modified Jethro structure promises some very attractive benefits:

UNLIMITED GROWTH POTENTIAL. I've discovered that the coaching of cell-group leaders is essential for continued effectiveness. The Jethro structure allows unlimited expansion of support systems for cell-group leaders.

BUILT-IN EQUIPPING OF LEADERSHIP. As leaders climb the ladder (or rather, descend it, as is the case with our topsy-turvy servant organizational structure), the cases which come before them increase in degree of difficulty (before they graduated, they simply passed cases too complex or difficult onto their immediate supervisor to handle). They are maturing as leaders, and soon they may have the opportunity to assume greater responsibility. New leaders always will be needed as the system grows to accommodate them).

The flip side of this dynamic is that for the leaders at the top (or bottom, whichever the case may be), only the cases of greatest significance—those requiring their refined leadership skills—remain for them to handle. No longer must they wade through the stacks of assignments far beneath their challenge level.

HIGH QUALITY CARE FOR THE PERSON IN THE PEW.   No longer is he or she simply a number. Now he is a face. He has a leader whom he must share with only nine other people, so he gets a significant amount of that person's attention. His problems are prayed for and worked on; if they are too difficult, they are passed on to someone with greater expertise. *Every problem gets solved. No one falls through the cracks!*

The Role of the Cell-Group Coordinator

Those supervising cell groups at the level of the coordinator or above must be concerned about fulfilling the following responsibilities:

CATALYZING STRATEGIC PLANNING.   Help cell-group leaders formulate their goals and plans, and monitor the implementation process. Encourage and affirm cell-group effectiveness and growth.

CONDUCTING ON-SITE CONSULTATIONS.   Attend a meeting of each cell group at least once each month. After the meeting, debrief with the leader personally. Help leaders to discern group and individual needs. Ask probing questions to enable the leaders to identify priorities and determine the next step to be taken.

EVALUATING GROUP BODY LIFE.   Guide leaders to facilitate the use of spiritual gifts in their groups. Ensure that, at a minimum, the four-fold functions are in place, and that each group is training and placing people in ministry in regard to their spiritual gifts.

SHEPHERDING THE CELL-GROUP LEADERS.   Pray consistently for each one. Also spend extended time in prayer seeking to determine from the Lord what should be the agenda of each huddle opportunity in your ministry community.

Build personal relationships with cell-group leaders. Make regular contact with them outside the context of this ministry community. Seek to determine their needs and how you can help them. Offer each leader personal encouragement and/or guidance.

Schedule periodic (at least quarterly) planning sessions with your cell-group leaders. Follow up on cell-group leaders after an absence from ministry community.

HELPING THE CELL-GROUP LEADERS CULTIVATE APPRENTICE LEADERS. Assist them in the process of identifying and investing in potential leaders. Hold them accountable to pray for and seek these leaders. Meet with all potential cell-group leaders and give them vision for future ministry possibilities.

Invite apprentice cell-group leaders to special orientation meetings and activities. Follow up to help apprentice leaders launch their groups.

You also should be responsible for seeking and praying for an apprentice coordinator or director who can be trained to replace you— or at least branch off Jethro style.

How Cell Groups Multiply

The Formation of Fishing Ponds

Carl George defines *fishing ponds* as events or gatherings at which cell-group leaders or apprentices can recruit members for their groups. We have found that certain individuals in our church are good at catalyzing the formation of middle-sized groups. This is the role of the C, or gatherer of 100, who is gifted at brainstorming and getting people in contact with one another. Fishing ponds may be neighborhood gatherings or block parties; barbecues or kite days at the park; or any kind of creative social function. Fishing ponds seek to link people to a cell group.

One of the best fishing ponds at CBC is the newcomers' class. This is a class designed to orient people to the church, help them make the decision to become members, help them determine their spiritual gifts, and place them in ministry. We have experienced a great deal of success by breaking the two-hour class into groups of four or five for half of the meeting, each under the direction of a cell-group leader or apprentice brought into the class specifically for that purpose. We scramble the groups for a few weeks so the newcomers slowly can find their niches, and then at the fifth week tell them to settle into their favorite group. Generally the Xa's then develop bonding relationships with their group by the end of the third week, which is the last week of new-comers' class . . . and, presto! They have a ready-made cell group of newly assimilated CBC members.

Using this method we have experienced as high as 75 percent assimilation of new members into cell groups. Our experience is that once people get a taste of cell-group life, they are very likely both to stay involved in cell groups and to become assimilated fully into the life of the church.

Each summer we have an event called CBC Bible Institute, which makes excellent fishing ponds for cell-group leaders. The Bible Institute is a series of high-accountability seminars led by gifted teachers on subjects ranging from doctrine and theology to book studies to topical studies dealing with finances or relationships. The perennial need for meatier teaching from the Word, which will surface in any church dedicating its worship services primarily to reaching the unchurched or feeding milk to the spiritual babes, is what gave rise to this ministry. Need-oriented cell groups will find a ready audience who are attracted to these teaching events.

There are many other possibilities of fishing ponds that facilitate new group formation. It could be a festival choir, special interest seminars, a weekend retreat, sports teams, and so on. These mid-sized groups function best as fishing ponds when they are ad hoc. Continuing groups tend to get crusty, making it difficult for new people to become involved. Ad hoc groups, with a definite beginning and ending, invite newcomers to join because group relationships have not stabilized yet.

It also is part of a cell-group leader's job to create fishing ponds for apprentices within the confines of his or her own growing cell-group, or among those to whom the group ministers. The leader must recognize that certain individuals within the growing group will develop affinities with the apprentice leader rather than with the cell-group leader. The Lord will use this process of bonding to facilitate the multiplication of the group at the end of your life cycle (which we will discuss later).

The Art of Multiplying Cell Groups

The topic of multiplying cell groups stirs great interest among cell-group members and leaders. Two dynamics in cell groups wage war one against the other. The first is the fact that multiplying a group is healthy for both the group and the kingdom. The second is the fact that, left to their own devices, very few groups ever would multiply. Multiplying is perceived as a potentially painful event, a split which severs relationships. People want to get together and stay together. They rarely realize that the group that closes in upon itself in this way will grow stale or die within one or two years. Multiplying is perceived as being unnatural.

One fun but revealing exercise to attempt with your cell-group leaders during your leadership support time is to ask for two volunteers to come up front, and give each a large, succulent orange. Instruct each to peel the orange and to divide it in half, but by using two different methods. Ask the first leader to divide his orange in half crosswise, along its equator. Ask the second leader to divide his on the north-south axis, along the naturally occurring segments. Then note what happens, and draw the parallel to cell groups.

A group ripped asunder without regard for the naturally occurring segments or affinity clusters within the group will make a big mess. If you split a group by arbitrarily counting off, or in this culture, even by using geographical boundaries or some means other than affinity clusters, you may end up with many injured group members. However, if you identify naturally occurring affinity or relational clusters within your group, plant a leader for each (or watch to see what leader naturally emerges to the top of each), and then divide the group by these clusters, the result will be much more beneficial.

To encourage the formation of these clusters, start early in the group's life to experiment with different cluster compositions. Perhaps allow your members to divide by their own devices into groups of three, four, or five members. Note who gravitated toward whom, and who took leadership. Try this for three or four weeks to see if any specific clusters are gelling.

You may wish to strategize group formation by drawing affinity maps. What groups of three, four, or five are most alike in the sense of similar lives? Who has kids with similar ages? Similar socioeconomic status? Similar interests? Perhaps previously developed friendships or networks of relationships? Or you may wish to use a combination of this method and the method described in the previous paragraph for structuring your clusters.

Clusters will be, in a sense, "mini cells." You will want to meet as a large group for most of the evening, but dismiss into clusters for special group exercises related to your Bible study, or for prayer or sharing. Develop the clusters with greater potential as your group progresses through its life cycle, for these will be your daughter cell groups. It will be very important to "release" leadership of these clusters to your apprentices, so that they may develop their own bonding with these cluster members and thus be prepared for group multiplication.

This also contributes to a higher quality of care within your group.

Many people will open up to smaller clusters of three to five when they would keep silent before a larger group. Linking people into a cluster means they will be missed more dramatically if they are not there. Their presence is needed and they will be touched by the cluster leader in such a way that makes it more difficult for them to move out of the sphere of influence of the group.

Coordinators should be in careful contact with leaders and be kept posted as to how apprentices are developing as leaders of these clusters. They should be given authority to give blessing or approval to the development of clusters, since these will be the care groups coming under this coordinator's supervision after the leader multiplies.

The Topsy-Turvy Church

To give cell groups their rightful place in your church will be to turn your church on its ear. It's critical to philosophically turn your organizational chart upside-down in order to help everyone realize the strategic importance of the cell-group leader's ministry. All other support functions in your church should exist to enable and equip the cell-group leader in the task of being a pastor to his or her group. Churches have been guilty of ignoring the potential of the lay leaders to be pastors to a group of their peers. In this regard, such individuals are similar to the customer service or sales representative in the secular business organization, of whom Peters notes:

> Ironically, the most lightly regarded people in most organizations, public or private, are those who are closest to the customer and most directly responsible for the quality and responsiveness of service delivered. This tradition must be reversed with a vengeance, if total customer responsiveness is to become reality.
>
> The care and feeding of the sales and service force—and more, turning them into innovators—is of monumental importance.
>
> Spend time with them; pay them well; recognize them; listen to them; empower them; train them; support them technically; hire (recruit) enough of them.[6]

Because it regards highly the people "closest to the customer"—the people in the cells—truly only a cell-group church can thrive on chaos—the chaos of changing human attitudes and relationships in a society more profoundly affected each day by future shock.

I don't know about you—but I am excited tremendously by the thought of a church where every need would be cared for, where the ninety-nine could be left safe in the fold to pursue the one who was lost (instead of vice versa), and where no one would fall through the cracks.

What potential such a church could have to reach a hurting world! What validation for the message of the cross—a message that says, "God cares for you, no matter how small you are."

The Lord Jesus, the Master Builder, wants to build such a church. And he wants to do it right where you are standing! Are you ready to begin pounding the first nails?

Action Steps

Evaluate your group structure.

Divide your weekend attendance by the number of groups. The ideal number should be eight groups per 100 people.

Examine the quality of your cell-group structure. Are each of the following needs being fulfilled?

Teaching—learning and applying God's Word.

Fellowship—building supportive, mutually accountable relationships.

Worship—praising God for who he is and what he has done.

Prayer—listening to and sharing intimately with God; interceding for others and God's work in the world.

Power—experiencing the filling and outpouring of the Holy Spirit.

Ministry—using spiritual gifts and loving each other in practical ways to meet needs.

Evangelism—impacting our society and sharing the Good News so that people become Christ's disciples.

Can your groups meet a diversity of needs in the community and the church?

Are your groups born to multiply—do they have a growth mentality?

Are your leaders free to innovate?

Do your groups have specific goals and time frames?

Are apprentice leaders in place at the inception of each group?

Are your groups exhibiting the four-fold functions of catalytic leadership, caring shepherding, growth-oriented evangelism, and environment-conscious hosting?

Evaluate your support structure.

What is the span of control in place over your cell-group structure? Do you have at least one coordinator for every five cell-group leaders?

Are your coordinators effectively:

Facilitating cell-group effectiveness by helping leaders set and evaluate goals; attending meetings periodically and debriefing and/or troubleshooting; helping leaders discern group and individual needs; helping leaders structure their groups according to spiritual gifts; building team spirit through quality ministry-community team time, prayer, and meeting time outside of ministry community with each leader?

Shepherding cell-group leaders by praying for each consistently; building relationships with each; scheduling extended planning times; and following up leaders who miss out on ministry community.

Cultivating apprentice leaders by helping cell-group leaders to identify and invest in potential leaders; meeting with potential leaders and giving them vision for future ministry possibilities; inviting them to leader orientation meetings; following up to enable apprentice leaders to launch their groups; and identifying those with gifts and/or burdens for target group ministries. Multiplying leaders by developing their own apprentices who can serve as coordinators.

Notes

1. Tom Peters, *Thriving on Chaos* (New York: Alfred A. Knopf, 1987), p. 27.

2. Ibid., p. 50.

3. Paul Yonggi Cho and Harold Hostetler, *Successful Home Cell Groups* (Plainfield, N.J.: Bridge Pub., 1981), p. 50.

4. "The Theological Basis for Cell Groups," *About Touch Outreach Ministries* brochure, p. 2.

5. These are available by writing: TOUCH Outreach Ministries, Box 19888, Houston, TX 77079.

6. Peters *Thriving on Chaos*, pp. 172, 175, 177–78.

Principle 7

Developing and Resourcing Leaders

You then, my son, be strong in the grace that is in Christ Jesus. And the things you have heard me say in the presence of many witnesses entrust to reliable men who will also be qualified to teach others.

2 Timothy 2:1, 2

Don Bennett is a Seattle businessman who decided he wanted to climb Washington's Mount Rainier. It's a stiff climb to the peak of the 14,410-foot summit, but so many individuals have made the climb that it no longer merits getting your name in the newspaper.

For Don Bennett, however, the climb was a remarkable achievement, and papers nationwide carried the news of the first amputee ever to reach Mount Rainier's summit.

In their book, *The Leadership Challenge,* Kouzes and Posner tell the story of how Bennett made the climb on one leg and two crutches. Asked to share the most important lesson he learned from his celebrated achievement, Bennett spoke of the team of individuals who helped him attain his dream, and commented, "You can't do it alone."[1]

The same can be said of building an effective church. Any church that seeks to be effective must mobilize a host of leaders who will team with the pastor to fulfill the church's goals. The number of leaders required is sizable. For cell-group ministry, at least 10 percent of the congregation must be trained as lay pastors, and that doesn't include the leaders needed for the other ministries in your church. Church effectiveness rises or falls on the quality and quantity of a church's leaders.

How do you recruit and train an ever-expanding core of leaders for your church ministries? How do you maintain morale and prevent burnout as they serve? How do you disciple your leaders so that their personal character grows and their ministry fruitfulness increases?

Kouzes and Posner interviewed five hundred outstanding business leaders to determine what they considered to be their most successful leadership methods. Five practices were common to each leader:

142

- Challenging the process
- Inspiring a shared vision
- Enabling others to act
- Modeling the way
- Encouraging the heart[2]

Make Leadership Development a Priority

If you want to cultivate a thriving church, you must make the care and feeding of your cell-group and ministry leaders the highest priority in your congregation. Lay leaders just don't drift into success; they need constant encouragement and training.

Ministry Community

CBC's leadership support event is called ministry community, a function absolutely essential to the existence of cell groups and our other key ministries (such as worship, child and youth programs, and community service projects).

Ministry community was pioneered at the inception of our cell-group thrust one and one-half years ago. It is a two-hour meeting scheduled every two weeks (except in summer), and is limited to care-group leaders, their immediate leadership (cell-group coordinators), and the leaders of other ministries throughout the church. Our first ministry community a year and a half ago was attended by about 40 people. Now almost 150 attend regularly.

VHS is an acronym Carl George coined which represents the threefold components of our ministry community:

VISION. The senior pastor gives inspirational vision in two ways: Vision must reaffirm core values by giving clear recognition to those leaders who are doing it right; vision must also focus future direction, for the church leaders need constant clarification of where the church is going.

Worship is often an important component of vision. A concentrated time of quality praise focuses minds and hearts on a track to minister and be open to what the Lord will teach. We usually devote thirty to forty minutes to the vision component.

HUDDLE. Here the cell-group coordinator has the opportunity to build the team of cell-group leaders in his care. These groups meet for forty to sixty minutes. They share, pray together, troubleshoot, and do some need-oriented teaching. In many respects the coordinators, who also have been accomplished cell-group leaders, use this time to model the dynamics that should be occurring in the leaders' groups each week. The huddle time is semistructured in that we provide guidance regarding what types of things should be happening, but the coordinators are free to determine their own agendas.

SKILLS. This component features structured times of skill training. We offer rotating skill electives in a seminar format, led by a team of gifted teachers. The objective is to equip leaders in a specific area such as need-oriented counseling, group ministry opportunities, skills orientation for new leaders, deepening your personal and group prayer life, leading group worship, selecting and training an apprentice, Bible-study methods, Christian doctrine, evangelism and assimilation, and growing and reproducing your group.

Obviously an activity such as ministry community takes a great deal of planning, energy, and other resources. However, the investment of these resources will pay enormous dividends in terms of the health of your church's ministries. Your willingness to invest substantial resources up front for the highest quality support and training for your leaders demonstrates your commitment to equip believers for ministry. Our cell-group structure would have declined or collapsed completely within the first six months had an effective leadership support and training activity not been in place.

There is a direct correlation between the energy that we put into ministry community and the fact that our cell groups are experiencing 100 percent annual growth. You'll find no easy path to growth—it always will take hard work.

Several years ago we became aware of a growing level of dissent among our handful of home Bible-study leaders. "We feel as if we're out here all alone with no support," they complained. They butted their heads against the wall for a few years, and then quit. They put in the work, but didn't receive the equipping from us to do the job right, the support, or the reward of seeing the fruit of their labor. Yes, ministry was occurring in the lives of the people in their groups. But it was only a shadow of what we now have with cell groups. Previously home Bible-study leaders were so stressed that we developed a time line by which we would predict, with a great degree of accuracy, when a given leader would burn out.

Now leader burnout may be a thing of the past. Some of our members who became cell-group leaders after leading home Bible studies were almost burned out on groups when we began the cell-group program. Today these same leaders are refreshed, revitalized, full of exuberance, and excited to see what God will do around the next corner! They are experiencing the fruit of their labors and seeing God work. Nothing is more invigorating than the sense of being used by God to accomplish his purposes. Our leaders are discovering, for the first time in their lives, the true joy and excitement of ministry.

Share the Vision With Your Leaders

True leaders know how to develop and live an enabling and empowering vision. Part of your role in developing leadership is to guide them through the process of developing vision. Tom Peters speaks about how effective leadership is marked by developing a consistent core philosophy, or set of values, as well as a vision of how the group enterprise will make its mark while embodying those values. The leader looks inward to refine and develop that vision continually, and then looks outward to seek to develop that vision in colleagues, customers, and anyone else who happens to get in the way!

Emotion

A leader soon will discover that a key part of living his or her vision simply will be the level of emotional energy that one is able to sustain. Followers are looking for leaders who can demonstrate continual enthusiasm, even when the chips are down. To the observer, evident emotion is the indicator of belief. In a period of doubt, followers study the face—and life—of their leader for signs of faith failure. For if the *leader* himself doesn't believe in this vision which is currently under attack, why should the rest of us risk our necks for it? But if the leader stands resolute in the face of opposition, the followers' vision will be strengthened. Peters says, "The vision lives in the intensity of the leader, an intensity that in itself draws in others."[3]

Focus

Many people are fine and analytical thinkers, and successfully can focus upon various concepts or projects. However, only a leader has that single-mindedness of focus necessary to keep the goals of the group ever before them. The leader eats, drinks, sleeps, and breathes the enterprise. If the enterprise fails, the leader fails.

Christ was a leader with a single-minded focus. Luke 9:51 says, "As the time approached for him to be taken up to heaven, Jesus resolutely set out for Jerusalem." He set his face toward his destination, and never swerved, even though everyone around him tried to distract his focus.

Storytelling

Christ demonstrated that leaders are master users of symbols and stories to communicate their vision. Christ spoke more often in parables than he did plainly, and reported a variety of reasons for this practice. Experienced communicators understand the power of a story or illustration to evoke an emotional, life-changing response in the listener or reader.

When he desired to demonstrate the process by which God's Word takes root in our hearts, Christ told a story involving a farmer planting a seed. All of his listeners, most of them poor fishermen or agriculturists themselves, easily identified with the frustrations of the individual trying to plant a field and encountering various adverse conditions: stony soil, weeds, and hungry birds. After their emotions were disarmed, they realized the story's double meaning. The adverse conditions which frustrated the farmer are similar to the adverse conditions that God encounters when attempting to plant the seed of the Word of God in the soil of our hearts!

You'll find the best stories in the daily events of life around us. As a leader, you are in the communication business. As a communicator, you must observe carefully and sift everything that you hear or read through the story sieve. Ask yourself, "What eternal principle might I use this story or event to illustrate?" Take a course in speed-reading, if necessary, and zoom through the newspaper, books, and magazines. Listen to informative talk shows or accomplished preachers on the radio and on television. Subscribe to a creative illustration service. Interview colleagues, friends, and acquaintances on any subject. Write down anecdotes and illustrations as you hear them. The stuff of stories is all around you!

Vision Casting

The process of fulfilling group goals, according to the authors of *The Leadership Challenge*, is very similar to the process of putting together a jigsaw puzzle. It's much easier when you can see the picture on the box. If you can see the big picture, you have a better idea of how the small pieces fit. Through storytelling, the more vividly the leader can paint a picture of the organization's future once its goals have been achieved, the easier it will be for the followers to recognize where all the pieces of the puzzle fit.

The advent of politics has made at least one worthy contribution to the process of communication: the stump speech. As a leader, you are constantly on the campaign trail. You are campaigning for the support, energy, and wholehearted participation of everyone in your organization. You will have countless impromptu opportunities to utilize many variations of the three- to five-minute stump speech for inspiring and imparting vision to your listeners. Peters recommends that you always "end the speech with a couple of examples of people in the ranks living the vision in their daily affairs—not in a dramatic fashion, but in a small way that illustrates the way the vision affects daily operating routines; try harder still to have that example encompass a small risk (not small to him or her) that someone took to enact the vision."[4]

Cultivating New Leaders

A biblical model for training lay leaders can be summarized in three words: *orient, involve,* and *equip.*

Orienting Lay Leaders

Matthew 10:1 relates how Jesus, after seeing the crowds and having compassion upon them, "called his twelve disciples to him and gave them authority to drive out evil spirits and to cure every kind of disease and sickness."

It's interesting to note that here is a group of guys who still had some very rough edges. They were from all walks of life—fishermen, tax collectors, and the like. They didn't undergo extensive training prior to this assignment. They simply observed Jesus, who modeled for them and then commissioned them with the authority to drive out evil spirits and heal diseases. He gives them some orientation throughout the remainder of Matthew 10 and in Mark 6:8–11, but no real training. Then he simply throws them into the water.

According to Luke 10, the disciples and their entourage returned, flushed with joy at the success of their mission. Mark 6:31 records that Christ called the disciples to ". . . come with me by yourselves to a quiet place and get some rest." (What a tantalizing passage for the overworked and burned-out pastor or church planter!) Luke then tells how they are debriefed by Christ, who puts what has happened in its proper perspective. Throughout the remainder of his time with them, he uses the principles they learned during this experience to help equip them for the powerful ministry that would characterize their lives in the unfolding of the Book of Acts and beyond.

The most effective process of training apprentice leaders is similar. Orientation for a potential cell-group leader at CBC occurs when a potential leader is assigned to a coordinator. The coordinator meets with the potential leader, assigns appropriate reading material, guides him through a copy of our cell-group leader's manual, and answers questions. The new leader also may attend special beginning skill training sessions at ministry community.

Involving Lay Leaders

The new lay leader is involved by being placed or confirmed as an apprentice in a cell group under an existing leader. The leader gives the apprentice various responsibilities in the group, one at a time, starting with the simplest first, and progressing until the apprentice has led an entire meeting, first under the leader's supervision, and then on his or her own.

In this way the apprentice learns by experience what he or she doesn't know. Training is need oriented; people learn best when they are motivated by their needs to seek resolutions to problems. After their leadership exposure, they debrief with their cell-group leader and/or coordinator.

Equipping Lay Leaders

We then begin the never-ending process of equipping the new cell-group leader, primarily through the teaching, team time, and skill seminars at ministry community, but also through individual meetings with the coordinator.

New cell-group leaders graduating from apprenticeship are supervised very carefully by coordinators, who help them plan and lay other groundwork for their new group. Coordinators contact these new recruits weekly, escalating this level of supervision to almost daily during the critical first few weeks of the new groups. Coordinators visit groups frequently and help troubleshoot afterwards.

As we recruit new cell-group leaders, we've found that one of the greatest hindrances to commitment is the fear that the new leader will be stuck out on his own. We seek to overcome this fear by demonstrating the high level of support given to leaders through the Jethro supervisory model and through ministry community, and by emphasizing that by becoming cell-group leaders they are making themselves a part of a team effort.

Encourage Risk Taking

In our quest to develop leaders, we must realize that true leaders are pioneers. They prefer not to follow established routes, but to step out into the unknown.

Pioneers are risk takers, innovators, and experimenters. They delight in nothing more than in setting challenging goals and finding new ways to achieve them. True leaders never can be satisfied with simply maintaining the status quo.

Tom Peters states:

> Today's successful business leaders will be those who are most flexible of mind. An ability to embrace new ideas, routinely challenge old ones, and live with paradox will be the effective leaders' premier trait. Further, the challenge is for a lifetime. New truths will not emerge easily. Leaders will have to guide the ship while simultaneously putting everything up for grabs . . . which is itself a fundamental paradox.[5]

The possibility of failure comes with the territory when you invest your resources in any true risk taker. If you have learned how to downhill ski, you will know the meaning of the ski instructor's quip: "If you're not falling, you're not learning." Many of the individuals we consider greatly successful—Walt Disney and his string of bankruptcies, for example—failed miserably numerous times. Soichiro Honda, founder of Honda Motors, said, "Many people dream of success. To me success can only be achieved through repeated failure and introspection. In fact, success represents the one percent of your work which results only from the 99 percent that is called failure."[6] Very few people unacquainted with the pain of failure ever will know the joy of true success.

This paradox may be most evident by observing the life of the Lord Jesus. Measured by the standards of someone wishing to begin a revolution, at the end of his life he was a miserable failure. A week before his death he was hailed as a conquering hero, but on his last night on earth he was betrayed and forsaken by his closest disciples. Gravely misunderstood and wrongly accused, he died the most shameful and torturous death the greatest empire in the world could contrive, with none to come to his aid. He who claimed to be King of the Jews was stripped of all his clothes and placed on display before those who despised him. He who said "Whoever comes to me will never thirst" (*see* John 4:14) died racked by thirst so desperate he gulped vinegar. He who had assured his followers, "I and the Father are one" (John 10:30), cried out, at the end, "My God, my God, why have you forsaken me?" (Matthew 27:46). For all appearances, the kingdom of him who said ". . . The kingdom of God has come upon you" (Matthew 12:28) now lay in tattered ruins as his disciples scattered and hid.

If you knew nothing else but this apparent defeat, you would have no choice but to conclude, with Isaiah, "He was a man of sorrows and acquainted with grief" (*see* Isaiah 53:3). You would be very surprised to hear such a man pray, mere hours before his betrayal, "I am coming to you now, but I say these things while I am still in the world, so that they may have the full measure of my joy within them" (John 17:13). You would be astonished to hear that such a man was ". . . the author and perfecter of our faith, who for the joy set before him endured the cross, scorning its shame, and sat down at the right hand of the throne of God" (Hebrews 12:2). You would recoil to see him exalted, by the hosts of heaven, as he who was:

> . . . worthy to take the scroll and open its seals, because you were slain, and with your blood you purchased men for God from every tribe and language and people and nation. You have made them to be a kingdom and priests to serve our God, and they will reign on the earth. . . . Worthy is the Lamb, who was slain, to receive power and wealth and wisdom and strength and honor and glory and praise!
>
> Revelation 5:9, 10, 12

In the upside-down kingdom, where strength flows from weakness, and exaltation from humility, so success springs forth from failure. Developing leaders means to be prepared for failure and to watch God turn failure to advantage for the kingdom.

Use Pilots to Innovate New Ministry

One important step in the process of training leaders is to encourage the use of pilots when innovating new ministries. A pilot is a trial balloon sent up to test for potential success or failure before full organizational resources are committed to the product or service.

How do you foster an attitude of innovation among your leaders? Recognize and honor any attempt to innovate, even if the result is failure rather than success, as long as the attempt is planned and implemented carefully. At CBC we present what we call the New Wineskin Award. In our ministry community setting, we present a gift certificate or some other small form of appreciation to leaders who have piloted new forms of ministry, whether they have succeeded or failed in the attempt. This encourages an atmosphere in which people feel supported in their effort to hear and follow the Lord's leading to new and more creative ministries.

Peters says:

> To speed action-taking—and reduce innovation cycle time . . . requires us to make more mistakes, faster. We must support failure by actively and publicly rewarding mistakes—failed efforts that were well thought out,

executed with alacrity, quickly adjusted and thoroughly learned from. We must personally seek out and directly batter down irritating obstacles—often as not small ones—that cumulatively cause debilitating delays and which champions cannot readily clear from their own paths.[7]

Most organizations tend to rehash abstract proposals constantly. Instead, the successful business or church of the future will be dedicated to substituting this theoretical approach with a piloting mentality. The testing of prototype services will be dramatically sped up to shorten the time between conceptualization and preliminary evaluation, which is a necessary prerequisite for adaptation in our age of chaos.

Build Supportive Relationship Networks for Leaders

After reviewing what more than five hundred executives reported as their most successful leadership methods, the authors of *The Leadership Challenge* felt they had developed an accurate one-word test to determine whether a person was progressing along the path to becoming a leader. That test involved that person's use of the pronoun *we*.

True leaders lead not from the front or from the rear, but from alongside. They are vested members of the team. Their use of the word *we* to refer to the team demonstrates their personal ownership of team goals.

Take a leader thus vested, give him the resources, and equip him with the necessary skills, and you have a person whom God can use in wonderful ways to do his kingdom work through your church. Peters stresses the importance of the axiom: "There are no limits to the ability to contribute on the part of a properly selected, well-trained, appropriately supported, and, above all, committed person."[8]

Leaders must be trained to mobilize the membership of your organization. When this has been accomplished you will see people using their gifts, equipped to do ministry, networking with others for accountability and resourcing, and enjoying their jobs! They'll stay at it longer and be more effective. As you develop these leaders they will see the benefit of developing and training others so that as your church grows, new people will be cared for and mobilized.

Placing Leaders in Effective Teams

There are two critical steps in the process of training leaders to mobilize your laity. The first is placing them in the right jobs and surrounding them with the right people. The skill of placing people with wisdom and discernment is one of the premier marks of a successful chief executive officer or senior pastor.

Placement is one of those pay-me-now-or-pay-me-later issues. Are you willing to invest the time and energy up front to ensure that you receive maximum benefit from each person's unique combination of working style, gifts, passion, and skills? Or would you prefer to spend three times the amount of time and energy later trying to mend the damage when things have gone sour?

Successful placement has four components.

FOCUS ON STRENGTHS.   Peter Drucker says the central question you should ask yourself is: "What are the strengths this person possesses, and how does this compare with the strengths required by the position?" At times you may need to eliminate someone on the basis of weaknesses. But the effective leader begins with strengths, not weaknesses. Interviews must be planned carefully in order to combat the interviewer's natural tendency to conduct interviews off-the-cuff, rather than recognizing them as a strategic opportunity for assessing a person's areas of strength.

FOSTERING COLLABORATION AMONG TEAM MEMBERS.   Your teams must be comprised of people who round out each other's gifts and skills. Each must be a team player who values the contribution of the others and understands his own role on the team.

Modeling the Way

The process of imparting leadership can be seen in 2 Timothy 2:1, 2: "You then, my son, be strong in the grace that is in Christ Jesus. And the things you have heard me say in the presence of many witnesses entrust to reliable men who will also be qualified to teach others."

Discipling leaders is a continuity which passes from one generation to the next. We see encapsulated in these two verses four generations, and the promise of others. It starts with Paul: "the things you have heard from *me*" and passes to Timothy: *"You* then, my son," to the third generation: "entrust to *reliable men*" in such a way that they may pass it to a fourth generation: "who will also be qualified to *teach others*." Paul here set up a progression which was intended to pass through all generations to the present day. It is your responsibility to pick up this progression and pass it to the next generation in such a way that they will be aware of their responsibility to pass it to the following generation.

Many times I have said, "Christianity is but one generation away from extinction." I don't mean that the Gospel of Christ is fragile, but that we are responsible to pass it on in such a way that each future generation may know the power of God, just as each previous generation had a role in getting it into our hands. Throughout history the ball has been dropped at least once. We thank God that his Word remained so that his Spirit could rekindle it in the hearts of men and women throughout church history. God has been faithful to pick up the pieces and to get the ball rolling again even after we have dropped it. But it is only because of his grace and mercy that we aren't floundering in darkness even in this present generation.

Yet his grace and mercy do not absolve our present responsibility. We must not drop the ball again. May it be said that our generation was faithful to equip the next in such a way that its members would be fully cognizant of their responsibility to pass the torch of God to the next generation after them.

Paul's words to Timothy reflect clearly the imperative to *model* the character and vision that God has given us. For he begins not with the cognitive aspect of our teaching, but with the way it is lived in our lives: ". . . Be strong in the grace that is in Christ Jesus" (2 Timothy 2:1). From this base of strength we may then proceed to the *entrusting* of the cognitive things to reliable men.

A woman in our church attributes her dynamic gift of teaching not to her mental preparation but to the fact that before she ever opens her mouth she has *lived out* the truth that she is teaching. "I am committed not to speak about something until the Holy Spirit first has demonstrated its truth in my life," she says. It is too easy for teachers to come up with an idea and then teach it as God's truth before we have experienced its reality in our lives. Whether or not he is gifted as a teacher, every leader is a teacher by virtue of the fact that God's principles are *modeled* in his life before the eyes of whom he leads.

Therefore, any change that God brings to the organization you are leading first will occur in the context of your life. Peters reflects this principle when he says, "It is quite simply impossible to conceive of a change in any direction, minor or major, that is not preceded by—and then sustained by—major changes, noticeable to all, in the way you spend your time."[9] When God reveals to you a door behind which lies a new opportunity for your church, the door to be opened is the leaders whom you are training; the keys to open it are the changes that God first works in your own life.

My experience as a pastor has made me realize the extent to which people are, as Peters says, "boss-watchers." This is particularly true when things are in flux and your church's operating conditions are ambiguous. "For better or worse, what you spend your time on (not what you sermonize about) will become the organization's preoccupation."[10]

One cell-group leader in our church told me about the time he had my wife, Janet, counsel his cell group to help them understand the particular assignment to which the Lord was calling the group. He had begun the group about a year earlier with the very clear sense that the Lord was calling him to assimilate newcomers to our church who wouldn't fit in anywhere else—to be a group for the fringe people God brought to our church. Throughout the year he quietly had proceeded about this task, and when Janet came to counsel them the group was full of such people.

As a result of this counseling process God led the group through, they clearly realized that God's assignment to them was to assimilate newcomers to the church—to be a group for the fringe people God brought to our church. Throughout this entire process, the leader says, "I sat silently in the background, watching as the Lord brought to my group members the realization that their mission was precisely the same as the one God had laid on my heart and I had been modeling for them."

Do you desire that your people develop a close walk with God, characterized by personal holiness? Then *you* must model this in your own life. Is your goal that they be generous stewards of the resources God has given them? Then *you* must be such a steward. Do you pray that they will live out body life principles in small groups? Then *you* must give your energies to molding small groups. Is your desire that they reach out to their neighbors in holistic disciple making? Then *you* must be a holistic disciple maker.

Peters also notes:

> Likewise, the proactive use of symbols, such as the sorts of stories you tell and the people you invite to meetings, sends powerful signals to the organization about what's important. The final confirmation of "what really counts around here," when things are changing, is who gets promoted—risk takers and harbingers of the new, or "the same old crowd."[11]

Even our smallest actions convey symbolic significance to those who are boss-watching. Don't ever catch yourself, in hindsight, saying, "But I didn't mean anything by that. . . ." Clearly think through your every action, because *everything that you do means something to someone who is watching you for an example.*

It always has been interesting to note the types of things reported in the Gospels, and especially when you realize that the Gospels are not an autobiography written by Christ himself, but a biography written by men who are looking from the outside into the life of Christ. Mark recorded that Jesus rose early one morning, doubtless treading softly so as not to awaken the disciples or anyone else in the house. At daybreak, he went to a quiet place to pray. Though this event sounds as if it might not have been too unusual for Jesus, someone noticed, and it now has a place of significance in the scheme of events that were formative in his early Galilean ministry, reported by someone who wasn't even among the twelve disciples (Mark 1:35).

Peters says: "Amidst uncertainty, when people are grasping at straws in an effort to understand the topsy-turvy world about them, their symbolic significance is monumental."[12] Christ modeled the importance of developing the inner person through time spent alone with the Father. And years later, as the disciples ministered, they would remember and experience the importance of this principle.

A crucial aspect of modeling the way is breaking down victories into bite-sized pieces. Don Bennett's victory wasn't that he reached the mountaintop in one glorious, monumental bound, but that he made it there one small hop at a time. Each of these steps doubtless was a battle. But each small step was a battle won, and it is the accumulation of many small battles gained that wins the war. Doubtless he lost a few battles—sliding backwards a few steps at a time on precariously balanced crutches. But even if you win three, and lose two, if this cycle is repeated long enough—and if you have the endurance—you will gain the peak!

Don Bennett's victory illustrates the importance of investing your energy and resources in applications-oriented small starts. Break a large goal into small pieces which easily can be conceptualized and as easily achieved, one at a time. Goal managing—the art of prioritizing the order and speed of these small bites so that you eventually may gain the peak—will justify your significance as an executive leader of your organization. Goal managing is how you will earn your salary!

If your church is to grow, you must establish a test-a-pilot program rather than a write-a-proposal mentality. The organization which spends its time sifting through proposals has no time for the one-at-a-time small steps that will gain the peak. To do a pilot is to take those small steps, and to learn the shortcuts that lead to the top.

Encouraging the Heart

The New Wineskins Award may be just one of the weapons in the arsenal of the savvy church leader who knows how to stroke leaders in just the right way. Results—those small steps—can arise only from a heart that is excited and encouraged about the task. This excitement then creates the right environment for the brain to order the feet to move. The inner resources to achieve Herculean objectives start deep in the heart believing that the goal can be obtained one small step at a time. Samson laid waste to a thousand men with the jawbone of an ass, but the only way he achieved this admirable feat was to thump one noggin at a time! The gift of God to such a man was not only extraordinary physical strength, but also the spiritual, mental, and emotional fortitude to envision such a large army of men laid waste with such a simple tool.

In addition to affirming your innovators, you'll also want to give constant affirmation to leaders who demonstrate:

- The art of intentionally training and releasing a plethora of apprentice leaders (we call this the Timothy Award).
- Creativity in reaching out and ministering to pre-Christians and/or recruiting new members for their groups (the Fisherman Award).
- Faithful care for straying group members who need to be won back to the narrow path (the Lost-Sheep Award).
- Endurance to minister to people over the long haul, even when at the point of exhaustion (the Second-Mile Award).

Even though you must recognize individual team players in this manner, the accomplishments of these players should be celebrated as team accomplishments. Several times each year you intentionally should schedule times of celebration just as the children of Israel celebrated intermittent festivals or feasts.

An example of this at CBC is our Thanksgiving celebration coinciding with the Thanksgiving holiday each November. This is the one time each year when our entire church body gathers together (we have to rent the valley's largest auditorium in order to fit in one place) with the express purpose of raising the roof. We sing, praise, pray, and remember the year's victories through a very moving multimedia presentation which affirms our unity primarily by showing slides of church members working together to achieve our objectives and by laying down pastoral vision for the coming year. Everyone leaves the celebration proud to be a part of the team and inspired to move ahead into the ministry that the Lord has for us in the next twelve months.

It may sound undignified to refer to the senior pastor as a cheer-leader, but it is a very important role. What would the spirit of an athletic event be like without cheerleaders? No doubt there would be some spontaneous applause because many individuals feel enthusi-astic about their team. But cheerleaders keep audiences at athletic events from looking as if they passively are watching television by organizing and coaxing expression of the enthusiasm felt by the par-ticipants. Enthusiasm is subject to the snowball effect. Unless it is expressed, it melts away into nothing, but as it gathers together and gains momentum, it escalates. The most effective cheerleaders re-hearse and prepare in advance the specific cheers they will use under various circumstances. Likewise, in order to build momentum and generate enthusiasm, you must have a strategic plan for building momentum at specific events.

The principle of cheerleading isn't reserved only for celebrations. You can practice cheerleading tactics whenever you are working with a team. Mervyn's, the successful clothing-store company, does this by encouraging its managers to write affirming notes to their employees on cards that begin with the positive message: "I heard something good about you." This should not be empty flattery, but an honest attempt to affirm and honor the employee's successes.

Peters demonstrates the importance of such affirmation when he says, "Success in today's environment will come when those one step from the line are honored as heroes, and empowered to act—period. A prime leadership task is to ensure that honor goes to the line and those who support it most vigorously."[13] This entire process requires an intensity and quality of communication between you and your leadership which is rarely experienced in churches. You must:

- Listen continuously.
- Take every opportunity to congregate. *Together* is the only setting wherein values can be transmitted.
- Freely share ideas and information.
- Quickly recognize and honor achievement.
- Celebrate as a team—both informally and formally—the small wins that represent the solid day-to-day performance of the majority of your work force.

The Church as God intends it to exist is not a casual, fly-by-night operation. It is a strategically planned, dynamic, and growing organ-ism in which extensive involvement of its members is the key ingre-dient to achieving and engendering the level of quality, service, and flexibility required to fulfill our objective of making disciples of all peoples.

Action Steps

Evaluate your present aptitude at developing and resourcing leaders. Are you:

Targeting a small group of individuals into whom you can pour your time and disciple-making energy?

Modeling for that group the character and skills that you would like to see instilled in them?

Releasing them for innovative ministry in an environment in which it's safe to fail?

In order to develop and resource your leaders more effectively, what changes do you need to make regarding how you spend your time?

How do you need to change the way that you communicate to others?

Do you have a consuming focus on developing reproducing leaders?

Do you present this as a crucial part of your vision at every level?

Identify your Timothys.

As your personal ministry, commit yourself to developing this inner core. When will you know that you have been successful?

Examine the path by which you currently identify and recruit talent for your church.

How can you make this process more intentional, more selective, more comprehensive—in short, watertight?

What life experiences—what challenges—are you giving to your leaders in order to develop them?

How do you debrief them after these challenges?

Do you have a regular ministry community support structure with a balance of these elements:

Vision
Huddle
Skill Training

Notes

1. James M. Kouzes and Barry Z. Posner, *The Leadership Challenge* (San Francisco: Jossey-Bass, 1987) p. xxiii.

2. Ibid., p. 8.
3. Tom Peters, *Thriving on Chaos* (New York: Alfred A. Knopf, 1987), p. 407.
4. Ibid., pp. 406, 407.
5. Ibid., 391.
6. Ibid., p. 259.
7. Ibid., p. 258.
8. Ibid., p. 284.
9. Ibid., p. 412.
10. Ibid., p. 410.
11. Ibid.
12. Ibid.
13. Ibid., p. 442.

Principle 8

Mobilizing Believers According to Spiritual Gifts

For by the grace given me I say to every one of you: Do not think of yourself more highly than you ought, but rather think of yourself with sober judgment, in accordance with the measure of faith God has given you. Just as each of us has one body with many members, and these members do not all have the same function, so in Christ we who are many form one body, and each member belongs to all the others. We have different gifts, according to the grace given us. . . .

Romans 12:3–6

Even though I had attended church since I was a child, it wasn't until I was a college student that I discovered the principle which has brought the greatest amount of freedom and release to my ministry.

As a busy college student, majoring in chemistry, with a full-time load at the University of California at Los Angeles, I also had an active ministry with the junior-high students at my home church. The task of discipling all these kids was immense, and I soon realized I couldn't do the job alone. Even if I had the time, I was not equipped adequately. I began searching the Scriptures to see if I had any alternatives to hari-kari.

Based on what I discovered in Paul's writings, I began teaching the principle of spiritual gifts and organizing ministry teams accordingly. The first fruit of this realization was Come Alive Week, a five-night summer outreach and discipleship program for junior-high students. Come Alive Week had been an annual event for several years, but when I took the helm, I decided to put into practice what I was learning about spiritual gifts. My leadership team was composed of college students. Together we studied spiritual gifts and sought to determine how each of us was gifted to serve, and then assigned ministry tasks in accordance with what we learned. To my astonishment, the ministry that I had dreamed might occur, had I had the time for it, began to occur without me! The results of that ministry still are evident today in the lives of those kids—now adults—who participated. Perhaps better yet, a group of college students came to understand that God had created them uniquely to fulfill certain aspects of a group assignment, and that working as a team, with each member making a valuable contribution in his own area of enjoyment, we realized our goals.

I believe the spiritual reformation begun by Martin Luther's Ninety-five Theses is a process which has continued through the present day. It has proceeded in phases. First was the realization of the direct approachability of God through our high priest, Jesus Christ. The Scriptures were placed back where they belonged, in the hands of believers, and translated so the common man could read them with understanding. The decentralization of the Church was another phase, and the rediscovery of the Great Commission another.

One of the few uncharted territories remaining in this spiritual reformation is mobilizing lay leaders for ministry. Although Luther steered us away from the centralized authority of the Church elite as the definers and owners of ministry, he was unable to complete that process to include the people in the pews. The church still makes a crippling distinction between the clergy and the laity, a distinction in which the clergy say, "We are the experts in ministry, trained in special schools called seminaries. Leave the ministry to us," and the laity acquiesce and say, "Okay. Minister to me." To placate them the clergy involves the laity in committees, boards, and social functions, but gives them no real license to minister.

Most churches pay lip service to the need to train their members, but don't allocate the resources or do anything serious about it other than to suggest that young people who really are committed to becoming ministers attend seminary. By the same token, most churches teach briefly about the biblical concept of spiritual gifts, but do little to help their members discover what their gifts are, and even less to help deploy them in ministries specifically using those gifts.

The typical American church has its usual ministries, established either on the basis of perceived need or simply because most churches have these ministries (such as Sunday school). These ministries need leaders. When a leadership vacancy occurs, the pastors or the ministry coordinators start calling their most willing (or susceptible) people: "We desperately need someone to take the third-grade class. This will be a real service to the Lord and our church. Will you do it?" The John

Doe whom they call may hate teaching, and particularly may despise third graders. In reality, his gift may be mercy. What would really excite him is hospital visitation. So one of two things will happen. He may capitulate and agree simply because he hasn't learned to say no and he knows he will feel guilty if he refuses. Once recruited, he will serve briefly but miserably in a job for which he is not equipped and has no heart. Or else he will refuse the position, and having incurred his church's disappointment for his perceived lack of faithfulness, eventually may become frustrated and hardened to doing any kind of ministry. Thus his involvement with the church will be retarded or reversed. This is a true lose/lose situation, and all because John is being asked to fill a role, with no regard for passion or giftedness, simply because the role exists and his is the nearest warm body.

But a church that truly desires to mobilize its laity for ministry must recognize:

- God gives equipping gifts for a diversity of types of ministry.
- Anyone can discover those gifts and use them in a ministry both personally fulfilling and highly valuable to the Church's mission.
- God raises up gifted leaders in response to our prayers *before* he asks us to reach out in ministry requiring that leadership.
- A church body is designed to function as a mutually dependent team, together discovering and fulfilling the assignment that God has given them.

My friend Dr. Don Weaver of International School of Theology tells the story of an associate working with the Christian-education program in one of Don's pastorates. "As I watched him in action and monitored feedback from him and others who worked with him, I discovered that he was unhappy with all the administrative details connected with his job. He could do them, but considered them a constant 'thorn in the flesh.' Yet he seemed to have a natural ability in counseling hurting people, though he was often criticized for doing this, because it wasn't part of his job description.

"The subject of spiritual gifts was just becoming popular at that time, so he and I did some studying together and discovered that he had the gifts of mercy and exhortation. I got the church leaders to agree to a modification of his job description, and we gradually moved him into a pastoral counseling role as he received training for this. His Christian-education responsibilities were phased out and given to two highly qualified laypeople, whom he trained.

"Several years later, after his training was complete, he opened up a family counseling ministry in the church."

My college experience with spiritual gifts helped me understand the importance of using gifts fully in the local church. When I began working with CBC I tried to ensure that spiritual gifts served as the foundation for our ministry, and sought to guide people into using their specific gifts in active ministry. It soon became apparent as we grew, however, that we needed to become more systematic in discerning gifts and placing people accordingly.

In the last few years as I have spoken to thousands of pastors in my seminars I have asked them, "How many of you have taught or preached on the subject of spiritual gifts?" Usually everyone raises a hand in response to this question. But my second question separates the philosophers (those who only talk about the right thing to do) from the teachers (those who take people from understanding to obedience): "How many of you have adopted a systematic approach that teaches all new members about spiritual gifts, helps them discern their gifts, and guides them into a ministry position in light of their gifts?" Very rarely has more than one out of twenty pastors raised his or her hand in answer to this second question. This survey confirms a condition that exists in far too many churches. One Christian leader expressed it so clearly: "Most Christians are educated far beyond their obedience."

If we know that implementing spiritual gifts is God's way for our churches to operate, and that it will free us to see true ministry occur among our members, why aren't we seeking to catalyze this among our congregations? It may be pride or ignorance, but more likely it is unbelief. Do we truly believe that God desires to work through those self-centered, immature saints who are the members of our churches? Do we believe that he will unleash them and release them to complete the process of building his church? I think most pastors or church leaders have been burned sufficiently that they are quite skeptical of the average member's capability. We mistakenly translate *realistic skepticism* to lack of faith in God to light a fire under those in our congregation to begin doing the ministry that God has called each of us to do.

The road to achieving a fully mobilized laity is a long and difficult one, but it can be traveled one step at a time. The first step is to take the biblical concept of spiritual gifts seriously enough to structure church ministry accordingly. Normally pastors and church leaders assume that teaching is the first step. Although pastors have been teaching about gifts for years, less than 5 percent actually guide people into ministries according to their giftedness. Completing this step *before* teaching about gifts will eliminate the placement gap.

The second step is to prepare the leaders necessary to guide people into appropriate places of ministry. At CBC we call these people spiritual-gift advisers or ministry-placement consultants.

The third step involves teaching your members the biblical concept of how spiritual gifts contribute to the proper function of a healthy body. Consistent teaching on the spiritual gifts helps believers understand how valuable they are to the church's health and growth. It enables them to discover what spiritual gifts God has given them, and motivates them to use those gifts in ministry.

The fourth and final step requires a supportive environment that focuses attention on the believer wanting to serve. So often pastors and church leaders recruit members to various positions without first listening to the individual and discovering what God already has placed on his or her heart. Not taking the time to listen first and provide wise counsel is one of the major mistakes made by pastors and church leaders. It causes people to feel used and unimportant. But a true disciple-making leader lovingly guides people into ministries appropriate to their giftedness, and then follows up to ensure that placement actually happens.

Implementing a Gifts-Based Ministry

Your goal is to implement a gifts-based ministry in your church. Before we examine the steps in greater detail, pray and commit yourself to putting spiritual gifts into practice in your ministry and in your church.

Step One: Organize

Church-growth studies report that in a healthy church in which a sufficient number of people are using their gifts in ministry, there must be 60 well-defined roles or tasks for every 100 adults attending worship. A church the size of CBC with 900 adults in worship needs almost 540 roles or positions. Many of these roles or positions are similar (in a church our size, we need about 80 to 100 cell-group leaders, all with essentially the same job description). In addition, if you seek to minister to children and youth (which is important if you want to reach families), you'll need teachers, greeters, administrative workers, social activity organizers and more. Consider the number of people needed to staff your worship service(s)—including ushers, sound people, worship leaders, set-up crews, and so on.

We haven't begun to scratch the surface. Think about all the community needs you could address if you sufficiently mobilized your members. God already has given you all the resources you need to fulfill your congregation's potential. Your greatest resource is *people.*

Have you done your homework by examining the various gifts that you believe God wants to demonstrate in your midst? Do all these gifts have ministry outlets? Have you written job descriptions expressing the potential ministry that God wants you to have if spiritual gifts were used as fully as possible? To embrace a gift-based ministry (and not just talk about it), you must recognize and write job descriptions for many, many positions—in a larger church, possibly as many as several hundred positions!

This is a good place to start. Evaluate the roles or positions necessary for the ideal functioning of your church to accomplish the ministry goals in your philosophy of ministry statement. Include a basic description of each position's purpose, what it will look like when that person is successful at fulfilling his description, what duties or functions that person is expected to fulfill, what resources the person will have at his disposal, what amount of time that person is expected to commit to, who he is responsible to and who is responsible to him, and what gifts or interests are needed or helpful for fulfilling this position. There is a sample job description as well as a job-description index by gift in Appendix V.

After you have written position descriptions and evaluated how many of each position are needed, add them up to ensure that you have an adequate number of positions. If you don't have 60 available positions for every 100 adults in attendance, ask God to challenge you in a deeper way to expand your ministry to the point where everyone in your church can find a ministry. As a shepherd, your job is to seek to equip everyone the Lord gives you to lead. You are responsible before God to create an opportunity for every member of your congregation to serve using his or her gifts. This is an absolutely critical part of the equipping and assimilation process.

Now that you have evaluated your situation from the standpoint of opportunities or available positions, the next step is to examine the equation from the perspective of existing gifts.

It is my experience that God supplies different churches with different sets of gifts. (Or perhaps people with certain gifts simply are attracted to certain churches where those gifts may be expressed.) It is important that you seek the Lord and commit yourself to using all the gifts that your theological perspective allows. Will you use the God-given gifts of the individuals in your church?

As you carefully study spiritual gifts from the Scriptures, I hope that God will be as gracious to stretch you as he stretched me to help me realize that he might want to gift people in ways that I never imagined—and perhaps sometimes even dreaded! He always does things in ways that we don't plan for or expect. If you are open and don't put God in a box, your church may experience some very exciting blessings.

If turned outward in service, your people's gifts may be used by the Lord to impact an unbelieving community, or they may be used to catalyze a lazy church to get serious in its task of reaching out and ministering to the unchurched. If your church is blessed with an abundance of people with gifts of service, helps, exhortation, or mercy, it has the ingredients to move out in sodalic ministry to the community, establishing mercy ministries, feeding the poor, or setting up an AIDS hospice or a home for unwed mothers.

Another step in the evaluation process is examining the work load of the professional ministry staff. Can some pastoral responsibilities be shared by other people? I have found laity in the church gifted to do almost everything that I as a professional pastor can do. The only exception, of course, are the top-level leadership functions like vision-casting, motivating others, and giving ownership of ministry. We should be developing those gifted in these areas as senior pastors of our daughter churches. I never have had to look very far to find people gifted in most other areas.

Sermon research and preparation is a good example. I was very tired of tackling alone the tremendous amount of work necessary to prepare a quality sermon when I realized that other people in the church might be willing to help. I spoke with our spiritual-gifts advisers and they quickly found several very capable people who lessened my load tremendously.

I am amazed by the things that some pastors spend their time doing. During one of my seminars I had just taught about the principle of spiritual gifts as it relates to delegation. Specifically, I stressed that the pastor shouldn't be the one to type the bulletin, order the Sunday-school supplies, and supervise the building maintenance. During the workshop, one of the pastors raised his hand and asked, "What if everything you do is something that only you can do?"

"Well," I replied, "that would be highly unusual. You would be the first person I've ever met who is so effective that nothing could be delegated."

Later I ate lunch with this brother, and what I discovered surprised me. He typed the bulletin, ordered the Sunday-school supplies, and personally supervised the building maintenance! Deciding to probe further I asked, "Why do you type the bulletin?"

He replied immediately and proudly, "That's easy. I'm the fastest typist in the whole church. I type one hundred and twenty words per minute." When I asked if anyone else could type the bulletin at the quality level required, he responded, "Sure, there is one woman who could do it, but she types only forty words per minute!"

I shared how he was robbing this woman of an opportunity to be productive for the kingdom of God by doing something that she could do as well (even if it would take her three times longer). Not only that, it was consuming his time so that he was unable to focus his energy and efforts on tasks that only he could do. This pastor returned to his church with a renewed vision and hope that the Lord could multiply his ministry if he utilized the gifted people already in his congregation.

If you're a pastor, equip your people to use their gifts. Make it a personal goal never to do anything that you can train someone else to do. You truly will be successful as a pastor on the day that you die and your thriving church continues ministering without missing a heartbeat.

Evaluating your ministry balance is the next step. You may be familiar with Donald McGavran's quantification of ministry type. *Class one ministry* is focused inward on the members of your own church, and *class two ministry* is focused outward toward the community. The critical issue is to evaluate the proportion of class one to class two ministry in your church. MacGavran says that, ideally, class two should comprise approximately 20 percent to 30 percent of the efforts of your church's work force.

A further step of evaluation to take after you determine your ministry ratios is how to redesign your church's class one ministry for greater class two impact. Most inwardly focused services have outreach potential. For instance, the nursery director could send letters of congratulations and invitation to new parents in the community.

Step two: Design Placement Process

The placement process involves guiding people with specific gifts mixes into positions in your church that will utilize those mixes.

If you want a more quantifiable view of the distribution of gifts, you can devise an inventory for your members to explore the types of things they like to do, the types of things they would do if they had time, and the types of things they are doing now. The Charles E. Fuller Institute offers four different kinds of spiritual-gift questionnaires from four different theological perspectives. If God has given a gift, people may not know what it is called, but it can be discerned as a result of these three avenues of exploration:

PERSONAL DESIRE.   The desire that God has placed in your heart may be an indication of a gift from God.

MINISTRY RESULTS.   When you use a spiritual gift, it accomplishes the intended purpose. When the gift of teaching is in operation, people learn. When the gift of mercy is used, people feel comforted. Evaluating ministry effectiveness provides guidance to an individual seeking to discover his or her gift.

CONFIRMATION FROM OTHERS.   This is perhaps the most valuable substantiation in exploring spiritual gifts. As others in the body see a gift in operation, affirmation helps give assurance and direction to a person seeking to uncover a spiritual gift.

No spiritual-gift inventory is fail-safe, but it is often a useful tool to help people in the discovery process. We have had much success using this test as a means to determine spiritual gifts in our newcomers' classes. The process of discovering gifts not only frees people from their emotional and psychological hang-ups about ministry, but also gives them a license from their church to proceed as God has gifted them.

At CBC, as I mentioned earlier, we use a placement system with specially trained people called spiritual-gift advisers. Advisers are specially equipped with teaching on gifts, our church's philosophy, and our structure of ministry. The advisers maintain an up-to-date data base on the job descriptions we mentioned earlier, and are well informed regarding the personnel needs of our church's various ministries. In order to graduate from newcomers' class, a person meets with a spiritual-gifts adviser. This adviser has before him the results of the advisee's spiritual-gifts test, and already has thought and prayed about the options available for placing such a person. During their brief meeting the adviser simply presents the options and helps guide the person into ministry. The adviser then serves as a link between the newcomer and the ministry leaders of the three ministries of greatest interest to the newcomer, ensuring that contact is made, a decision is reached, and actual service has begun.

Other churches take different approaches to the placement process. A smaller church may be able to use an approach which is far less structured but equally intentional. But as a church rises above 300 members it has an increasing dependence upon effective systems.

Follow-up is a crucial part of this process. People's interests change, and I believe the spiritual gifts given them by God also may change. Numerous times one of our members has gained a particular additional spiritual gift—usually because he needed it to minister effectively in a specific situation—simply by praying steadfastly for that gift. We must recognize the need for people to move in and out of various areas of ministry, and we must be prepared to recognize when they have graduated from a ministry and reorient and place them in another ministry. Frequent and clear communication between your spiritual-gifts coordinator, advisers, and your ministry leaders is the only way to keep current on your members' changing ministry involvement needs.

The church with a serious commitment to spiritual-gifts-based ministry also may develop specialists who move like itinerant teachers among the various cell groups and other groups in the church, doing ministry-involvement counseling. My wife, Janet, has had this role at CBC. God has given her the remarkable ability to spend a session with an entire group of people and help them to realize the unique gifting or ministry assignment that he has given them as a group.

You'll need to recruit one or more people to serve as counselors to help guide people into appropriate ministries using their gifts. If you need help training these people, the manual *Spiritual Gifts Implementation*, available from the Charles E. Fuller Institute, contains the organizational guidance to identify and train these people.

Step Three: Teach and Guide People Into Ministry Positions

How do you determine peoples' gifts? One way is to ask people, "What do you like to do? What presses your happy buttons? If you could do anything you desired in order to help people, what would that be?" Many times people who are responsive to the Holy Spirit already are exercising their gifts even if they can't identify their gifts yet. Those with the gift of intercession may not know they have it, but they enjoy praying so much that they already are doing it the way an intercessor would do it. Those with the gift of hospitality are entertaining visitors and making their home a comfortable place for others. Those with the gift of teaching already may be teaching Sunday school. If people seem to do what they're doing well, and are enjoying it, they likely are gifted to do it.

Use a variety of settings to teach about spiritual gifts. We use three basic approaches—newcomers' classes, various small-group studies, and special advanced spiritual-gifts workshops.

Newcomers' classes are the entry-level point for teaching about spiritual gifts. What are the various gifts expressed in the Bible? What are their characteristics? What will the person who exercises these gifts do well? Our precedent in this teaching is the Apostle Paul, who spent much time (particularly with the entry-level Christians at the church at Corinth) discussing the appropriate use of gifts. Effective teaching at the entry level has a very freeing effect upon Christians who come to realize that they indeed are equipped specially for an important role in the body of Christ.

Make sure that you implement your placement procedure you designed in step 2. This is crucial for effective mobilization.

Special ongoing studies also are needed to continue the education process after a church member has graduated from the newcomers' class. These studies can be worked into sermons, ministry community events, special seminars for leaders, or special training classes similar to our six-week summer teaching events called CBC Bible Institute.

Step Four: Ongoing Development

Training in using spiritual gifts should not end after placement. The greatest development naturally will occur under the supervision of ministry coordinators as an individual is oriented, evolved, and equipped in ministry skills. Ongoing development involves holding ministry coordinators accountable to ensure that individuals under their supervision are developing progressively.

Advanced spiritual-gifts workshops also may be useful to further evaluate and develop spiritual gifts. One goal of these workshops is to ensure that people are paired with mentors who share their gifts.

Some time ago we realized that we needed to provide advanced, ongoing training for people in areas of their spiritual giftedness as a part of the equipping process for which we were responsible. Two primary needs of our church at that time were for quality administration and intercession. We were operating with a moderately large congregation (almost 1,200) in a very small facility (a single auditorium seating 400, and limited classroom space on five acres of land) with limited resources (our church was relatively new and our congregation relatively young, so our financial base was still tenuous). Our great need was for quality programming administered efficiently and creatively. Staff members of churches with exponentially greater facilities but smaller congregations frequently have visited our church and expressed shock that we were able to accomplish so much with such scanty resources.

Second, the crucial developing need of our church was (and now is) for quality intercession to solve some critical problems. A very large percentage of our congregation is previously unchurched, and our body has many serious personal needs. In addition, we were at a critical juncture where our limited facility was beginning to constrict our growth potential and demand. We desperately needed some God-given insight regarding how to address these issues and allow our growth to continue unabated. And finally, we were at a critical transition point as a result of my job change to CRM and the need to restaff. The predominance of the intercession gift meant that all our problems could be bathed in quality intercessory prayer, and obstacles which otherwise could negatively affect CBC's momentum are being removed as the church surges ahead.

A gift-based approach to ministry helps develop tolerance, mutual respect, and interdependence among the body. Don Weaver tells about another young man in his church who used to be quite critical of people who simply walked past what he considered to be an "obvious need"— overflowing wastebaskets, a toy not in the toy box, where it belonged, a lawn mower out of gas, and so on. When this young man learned about spiritual gifts, he became aware that his own gift was serving to meet the practical needs of the body. Don says, "He also gained the insight that he was viewing and evaluating others in the body through his own giftedness. He expected them to see what he saw and be sensitive to the needs he detected and then to 'do something about them.' It was a good experience to watch his criticisms subside and his appreciation for others in the body increase." A gift-based approach to ministry helps develop tolerance, mutual respect, and interdependence.

Spiritual gifts can be such a treasure chest of opportunity that you will wonder how you ever did without them. They will free people to

serve the Lord as he has called them, and to experience the fulfillment
that comes with obedience.

Action Steps

Evaluate your available or needed positions or roles.
Do you have at least 60 roles available for every 100 people in attendance?
Write job descriptions for all roles or positions.

Evaluate the prevalent gifts in your church.
List the biblical gifts which should be used in your church.
Compare this list to the reality of what gifts are being used.

Evaluate your ministry ratios.
*How much ministry is class one and how much class two? How can you
redesign class one ministry to increase outreach?*

**What process will you use to teach consistently on spiritual gifts in
a way that helps people discover, develop, and use their gifts in
ministry?**

What system will you use in your church to close the placement gap?
Newcomers' classes? Small groups? Spiritual gift workshops?

Who in your church could serve as spiritual-gifts advisers?
What training to do they need, and how will this training be accomplished?

What advanced spiritual-gift training technique will you employ?

Principle 9

Appropriate and Productive Programming

Not that I have already obtained all this, or have already been made perfect, but I press on to take hold of that for which Christ Jesus took hold of me. Brothers, I do not consider myself yet to have taken hold of it. But one thing I do: Forgetting what is behind and straining toward what is ahead, I press on toward the goal to win the prize for which God has called me heavenward in Christ Jesus.

Philippians 3:12–14

Peters notes five areas of management which will be characteristic of businesses that thrive into the next century:

- An obsession with responsiveness to customers.
- Constant innovation in all areas of the firm.
- Partnership—the wholesale participation of and gain sharing with all people connected with the organization.
- Leadership that loves change (instead of fighting it) and instills and shares an inspiring vision.
- Control by means of simple support systems aimed at measuring the "right stuff" for today's environment.[1]

Who is the customer of your church? For the church that exists to make more and better disciples and thus do its part to fulfill the Great Commission, the customer is the pre-Christian. The Church of the twenty-first century will be one which is *acutely responsive to the needs of the potential disciple.*

The Purpose of Programming

Programming is simply the means your church employs to bring about its ends—to make more and better disciples. Rather than programming being an end itself, as it is in most churches ("Why do you have a Sunday school?" "I don't know. Don't most churches have

Sunday schools?"), programming should be the result of your attitude of responsiveness to your customers—to your potential disciples.

This means that programming is both appropriate and productive. These two words address the quantitative and the qualitative issues related to programming. Quantitatively, programming is limited to that which is essential to help your church achieve its qualitative objective: making more and better disciples.

In too many churches, programming proliferates because there is no focused goal by which to evaluate existing programs or proposals for new ones. Programs are begun simply because they meet some need of some of the existing members. For example, the social committee in many churches is an extremely resource-intensive program designed to fulfill the nebulous function of someone coordinating things whenever somebody feels the need to have a social event—regardless of rationale.

In the *effective* church, on the other hand, customer-oriented skill building is the name of the game. All programming, whether current or proposed, mercilessly is subjected to the question: "How will this help us develop our customers into more and better disciples?" Strategic programming seeks to:

- Equip leaders with problem-solving skills so they may achieve consistent quality improvement.
- Equip leaders with *naive listening* skills in order to better understand the intangible attributes of a product in the customer's eyes.
- Empower front-line sales and service people to solve (or more fundamentally, to *want* to solve) most problems on the spot, rather than buck them or blame them on the system.
- Treat every customer as a market segment with special needs, as well as someone with whom we wish to develop a lasting relationship based on the unconditional love of Jesus.

Obstacles to Effective Programming

Lack of Clear Ministry Values

Our values are statements of what is truly important. Whether or not they realize it, most pastors and church leaders operate from a subconscious set of convictions and priorities. Your values shape your understanding of the church's mission and influence your involvement throughout the planning process, especially during the implementation phase. If a church attempts a planning process without taking time to identify important individual and congregational values, people's differing assumptions almost always lead to program ineffectiveness and interpersonal conflict.

Recently when I was eating breakfast with Jim Dethmer, pastor of Grace Fellowship Church in Baltimore, I asked him, "What are your key values?"

Jim responded, "Personally, I have three major values that shape my life. The first is the priority of worship, both personal and corporate. The second is the importance of reaching lost people by spending lots of time with them. The third is the value of effecting life change in people through a fresh encounter with Scripture."

If you were familiar with how Jim spends his time, you would understand how the three statements he made accurately reflect his core values. As founding pastor Jim also has woven these values into the fabric of Grace Fellowship Church.

As I examine my own values, it is apparent that I consider the process of equipping, training, and resourcing leaders to be of utmost importance—especially for those who are church planters. That's primarily why I moved from pastoral ministry at CBC to apostolic ministry with CRM. I also seek to develop new and better ways to carry out ministry; thus I deeply value innovation. If given a choice of doing something the way it always has been done and venturing to do something in a new way, I'll choose the new approach every time (even though it may not always work).

Churches also have organizational values. For instance, some congregations are very reluctant to take programming risks. If you were to review the minutes of the governing board of many churches, you would find that the safe, conservative route consistently is chosen. The basic standard is demonstrated by the seven last words of the church: "We've always done it this way before"—or by its corollary—"We've never done it this way before." Tradition is the primary definer of ministry and the justification for rejecting new ideas.

How does a church discern its core values? Examine how it spends its time and money. These are the two most accurate indicators of what is important to an individual or to a congregation. *Regardless of what you say you believe, what you do with your resources is the true measure of your convictions and priorities.* If someone were to examine your church calendar and budget, what would he or she conclude about your values?

Many resources have been published to help you determine your church's values. Edgar H. Schein's book, *Organizational Culture and Leadership*, published by Jossey Bass, presents an in-depth process for uncovering organizational assumptions and core values. Chapter 10 in particular deals with how leaders imbed values into a group and transmit culture. Another resource is John Sculley's outstanding book, *Odyssey*, published in 1987 by Harper and Row. *Odyssey* tells the fascinating story of Steven Jobs and his establishing one of the most rapidly successful corporations in history, Apple Computer. A third resource for those serious about church values is Hans Finzel's doctoral dissertation, "A Descriptive Model for Discerning Organizational Culture," available from Fuller Theological Seminary in Pasadena.

Lack of an Intentional Approach to Ministry

The first place this lack is evident is in the goal-setting and budgeting processes. Many churches lack a clear sense of ministry values and direction. Thus the planning process is haphazard or unfocused.

In the organization that is adaptive and flexible to change, the planning process is a fluid one. Each year you should see substantial modifications not only to the content and format of your overall plan, as embodied in your stated goals and objectives, but also to the planning process itself.

Another place that lack of intentionality reveals itself is in the manner in which one measures success. How do you know when your leaders have done what you asked them to do? Do you have a vision which encompasses specific results, or is your vision limited to a set of vague ideals?

Intentionality means you will require a specific ministry proposal by which to evaluate every new idea for a ministry program. The following outline of what every proposal should contain is from the *Pastor's Planning Workbooks*.[2] An effective proposal must include:

- *A statement of purpose* for the proposed program.
- *Details on measurable results*—how the program will be evaluated to easily determine whether it has achieved or is achieving its purpose.
- *A proposed plan*—what specific steps are required in order for the program to achieve its purpose.
- *Required leadership*—outline what abilities will be needed, what training will be required, and be specific about what leadership now is available for successful operation of the program.
- *Support personnel*—what other resources (lay people) will be needed to make the plan work, and an assessment of who is available.
- *Facilities*—what other resources (building, equipment) will be needed to make the plan work, and an assessment of what is available.
- *Budget*—what other resources (money) will be needed to make the plan work, and where it will originate.

Lack of Ownership of Ministry

This occurs when one of three conditions exists: First, conflicting values are present in the congregation. (Refer to the above discussion on ascertaining core values.) Second, people are not involved adequately in the program's planning process. Most people want to be involved in designing programs that they will be asked to support. Pastors who choose to ignore the key opinion leaders in their congregation during the planning process are asking for trouble.[3] Third, the ministry itself is not addressing the felt needs of the people for whom it was designed. People working in ministry soon will sense if what they are doing—even if they are giving it their best shot—counts in the scheme of things. They also will know the value of their input regarding how the ministry operates. If you don't take people or their ministries seriously enough, your co-workers will become opponents and you will find that your church is, at best, simply taking up space and wasting time.

Lack of Excellence

Tom Peters emphatically states that the effective organization first must have a "quality revolution":

> A quality revolution means eating, sleeping, and breathing quality. Management obsession and persistence at all levels are essential. But the passion must be matched with a detailed process. And, always, the customer must be present—as the chief definer of what's important.[4]

Peters herein defines two elements which must be present in order to have a quality program—both a *passion for quality* and a *system for ensuring quality*. Both elements recognize that quality improvement is a process with no upper limit; as Peters says, "There is no such thing as a top-quality product or service. All quality is relative."[5] You can be the best, but you never can be the best you can be. This is good news for leaders who must recognize that to say "we have arrived" is anathema to the health of any growing organization. To grow and improve is always to have a higher mark for which to aim. From any point—whether high or low—on an open-ended scale, *one can always progress*. Herein lies the essence of hope and inspiration: "Things always can get better."

A key technique in the search for excellence, which very rarely is practiced on either an individual or an organizational level, is to underpromise and overdeliver. Too many pastors and churches make big promises about the needs they are going to meet and their customers' quality of life if they only will "come along for the ride." Christ, on the other hand, at times almost seemed to attempt to discourage potential disciples from following him. Luke 9 relates how, as Christ was heading through Samaria toward Jerusalem for his rendezvous with the cross, he encountered a string of potential disciples. One was unsolicited: "As they were walking along the road, a man said to him, 'I will follow you wherever you go' " (Luke 9:57). Sounds like a pretty good prospect, eh? Christ's response seems intended to discourage (or at least to sift): "Foxes have holes and birds of the air have nests, but the Son of Man has no place to lay his head" (v. 58). Christ saw through to the man's true gods—perhaps in his case, security or being accepted by peers—and, as usual, challenged him to submit to Christ's demand for absolute lordship in his life. We are not told whether this particular man accepted the challenge.

To another, Christ gave the simple command: "Follow me" (v. 59). But the second fellow objected, "Lord, first let me go and bury my father" (v. 59). Sounds like a reasonable proposal. God surely doesn't expect us to leave dead family members lying around! Yet once again Christ saw through and addressed the challenge to his lordship: "Let the dead bury their own dead, but you go and proclaim the kingdom of God" (v. 60).

A third stipulated, "I will follow you, Lord; but first let me go back and say good-by to my family" (v. 61). In this man's case, Christ saw that the enemy was the double-mindedness of committing to do something, and then changing his mind. Christ's answer gives an important clue to the nature of ministry and the basis for selectivity of leadership: "No one who puts his hand to the plow and looks back is fit for service in the kingdom of God" (v. 62). Low-commitment leadership is intolerable in ministry.

Christ did not overpromise. He didn't advertise his program in glitzy headlines reading: "Follow me and you will have peace and joy forevermore." And yet, peace and joy forevermore were precisely what he delivered. The value of what Christ delivered was so evident to the eleven apostles who succeeded him that ten of them faced untimely deaths while filled with unswerving joy!

Peters noted several examples demonstrating the value of this principle. Airlines are notorious for overpromising and underdelivering. When you are sitting in the plane on the runway and hear the flight attendant announce over the intercom, "There will be a ten-minute delay before takeoff," you automatically interpret this as a code phrase whose true meaning is either "the plane will be an hour late" or "we don't have the foggiest notion when, or even if, this plane ever will leave."

Had the flight attendant announced, "Folks, we're sorry, but it looks like we'll be sitting here for another forty-five minutes," and then thirty minutes later the plane took off, everyone in the plane would have spent the flight rejoicing that they had been given a wonderfully precious gift of fifteen minutes by the airline!

Christ told of a man who had two sons. The first he told, "Son, go and work today in the vineyard." The son replied, "I will not," but later changed his mind and went.

Meanwhile the father went to his second son and made the same request. This one answered, "I will, sir," but then did not go. Christ asked, "Which of the two did what his father wanted?"(Matthew 21:28–31). The first son underpromised and overdelivered.

The need for integrity in the ministry today is obvious. Even society itself is demanding greater accountability of religious organizations. As Christian leaders, we must demand total integrity of those we are developing. Tom Peters calls this "the Boy Scout/Girl Scout/ 'squeaky clean' sort" of integrity where, in all dealings with people and systems, inside the organization and out, you set "absurdly high" standards for integrity and then live them out with no room for gray.[6]

Lack of Finances

A lack of finances might have one or a combination of the following three causes.

The most common is a *lack of ownership of ministry*. What people help shape, what they invest a piece of themselves in, they will support with their time, money, and energy, because they become directly responsible for its success or failure.

Lyle Schaller addresses the issues of stewardship and finances in a helpful book called *44 Ways to Expand the Financial Base of Your Congregation*.[7] He perceives two other problems. First, the need for funds is not adequately or thoroughly communicated to those in the position to give; and second, your leadership is not perceived by your congregation as being trustworthy in handling their money!

Many churches that either are young or cater to particularly young audiences also struggle with finances simply because their members have not yet had sufficient time to build a strong financial base. Such has been the case with CBC, which has operated for a relatively short time in a community where young families with low capital are forced to buy expensive homes and therefore make high monthly mortgage payments.

Lack of Ministry Space

This phenomenon is known to church-growth people by the term *sociological strangulation*. It is a common problem which simply means that you have a wooden shoe too small for a growing foot. Sociological strangulation can occur in one of four areas: worship space, education space, parking space, or administrative space.

Because of the 80 percent rule, many pastors don't diagnose sociological strangulation until it is too late. Looking at the congregation, they see some empty seats, and they think, "We still have a little way to go before we're completely full." In reality, if more than 80 percent of your seating, Sunday-school, or parking capacity is filled, then you already are full. A newcomer walking into an auditorium which is more than 80 percent full generally will turn away rather than expend the energy to locate a seat in a part of the auditorium which is not his favorite and may be difficult to reach.

There are three basic solutions to solving space problems. Perhaps the easiest is multiple services. By adding more worship services (along with expanding the children's Bible-class program), CBC grew to accommodate 1,200 people in an auditorium that seated only 275! Another option is building or leasing more space on the present site (auditorium, classroom, or parking). Some churches do this one step at a time by installing modular or temporary facilities. The most challenging is relocating to another site which can meet the space needs.

Organizational Strangulation

This barrier can be expressed in several ways. An unwillingness to change can be expressed by overmanagement. It is as tempting for churches as it is for any other organization, private or public, to bureaucratize—that condition in which boards and committees seek to control and restrict rather than release and encourage. In this situation, any attempt at innovation by the church's members (starting a new home fellowship group, for instance) may be met with, "We're not necessarily opposed to the idea, but you have to go through the proper channels." *Proper channels* is a code almost always indicating the way by which those *in power*, whether professional or lay leaders, seek to control and restrict.

Peters reports,

Excessive organizational structure is a principal cause of slow corporate response to changed circumstances. We must—1) radically reduce layers of management (no more than five layers as maximum in any sized firm); and 2) limit layers in any one facility to three at the most.[8]

The role of middle manager in this three-layer cake becomes the most important, but, Peters says, it must be completely changed from the traditional concept of this role. Middle managers must enter into the coaching function, rather than being controllers. *Equipper* and *controller* should be antonyms in this usage.

Bureaucracies also tend to favor *efficiency* (doing things right) over *effectiveness* (doing the right things). They have inflexible, standardized measurement systems, and those individuals who are the only ones in a position to make quick and accurate value judgments on the issue of services which should be rendered have no authority to do so and therefore little ownership.

Why is it that the most dynamic organization on earth, the Church, so often is the least willing to change? How can we design and implement a planning process that will encourage innovation, uncover opportunities, and release people for greater ministry?

A Strategic Planning Process

The planning process of the average church is poorly conceptualized and even more poorly executed. But properly implemented, a strategic planning process provides both the direction in which a church should move and the energy to get it started.

Strategic planning is defined by Pfeiffer, Goodstein, and Nolan as "the process by which the guiding members of an organization envision its future and develop the necessary procedures and operations to achieve that future."[9]

The assumption behind strategic planning is that many aspects of that future can be influenced or changed by actions you can take today. For the Christian this is not simply projection-based planning, but realizing that through prayer and our relationship with God, we can be a catalyst to help bring about a future in alignment with his will.

Even though it is not written from a Christian perspective, the *Applied Strategic Planning Model* is the most effective, biblically consistent model I have seen. It represents a process-oriented, systematic effort to deal with the inevitability of change and to attempt to envision a future which utilizes change to the pastor or church leader's advantage. The following steps are adapted from *Strategic Planning*, for application in churches.[10]

Plan to Plan

COMMITMENT.   Without the enthusiastic involvement of the senior pastor and key lay leaders, any planning process is doomed to failure. Some pastors and church leaders view planning as unspiritual, expressing their well-intentioned desire instead simply to "let the Spirit lead." However, nothing is more spiritual than planning, which is making a statement about the future. In Christian terms, it is seeking to discover and express faith in God's will. Paul writes, "Be very careful, then, how you live—not as unwise but as wise, making the most of every opportunity, because the days are evil. Therefore do not

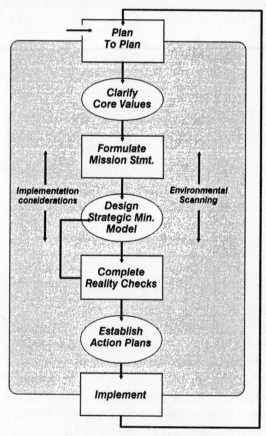

Applied Strategic Planning Model
(Modified for churches by Robert E. Logan)

be foolish, but understand what the Lord's will is" (Ephesians 5:15–17). The pastor must demonstrate that he or she values the process of discovering God's will by investing personal time and energy in a way that is visible to the congregation.

IDENTIFICATION OF YOUR PLANNING TEAM.   If you are planting a new congregation, your initial planning team simply may be comprised of you and your spouse. But leaders of established congregations must identify a strategic planning team to oversee the process so that everything comes together as it should. A working group of four to seven people is usually most effective. Ensure that this team has one or two visionaries, networkers, administrators, and key opinion leaders. Also be sure key areas in your church's ministry (such as, worship, children and youth ministries) are represented on the planning team. Since this group will seek to involve other people at all levels in the congregation, the choice of the coordinating team is very important and must be bathed in prayer.

TIME.   Strategic planning almost always takes longer than anticipated. The process in a church ideally takes nine to twelve months to complete. But snags will arise, and these obstacles must be faced, and not put on the back burner. Each of these challenges must be confronted and resolved before the planning process can continue. The strategic planning team should meet for an extended period at least monthly throughout the planning process. Meeting at a location away from the normal interruptions of ministry is ideal.

Clarify Your Core Values

This step makes this model very different from other planning models. As stated earlier, your values shape your understanding of the mission, as well as every aspect of the planning process, and particularly the implementation phase. This is the point at which you define what's important, then set convictions and priorities for your church's life and ministry. A *values audit* is both the most important and the most difficult part of the planning process.

PHILOSOPHY OF MINISTRY.   Your philosophy of ministry is the way your church approaches its work. It clarifies your assumptions about how ministry occurs and the way in which decisions will be made. For example, at CBC, our philosophy of ministry dictates that we would rather risk offending the churched person than losing the unchurched person. So we will risk a little rock'n'roll in a worship service, and we won't display traditional symbols of churchiness (choir robes, hymnals, lectern, and so on).

STAKEHOLDER ANALYSIS.   A *stakeholder analysis* is an examination of your church's relationship with individuals, groups, and organizations who will be affected by or interested in your strategic plan. Certainly the members of your church are interested, but what about potential disciples who are not yet a part of your congregation? Remember the importance of researching your target group to determine their attitudes, interests, and needs. Peter Drucker, the father of modern management, says, "The need to research the people who should be customers but aren't is, of course, preached by every marketing text. But few businesses actually do it."[11] What is true of businesses is even more true of churches! If you haven't done so already, get out into the community and do some naive listening.

Formulate Your Mission Statement

Three questions must be addressed during this phase of the planning process:

WHO?   This clarifies the target group that you are seeking to reach.

WHAT?   This usually is stated in terms of services or products offered, but strategic planning experts tell us that it's far better to identify the needs that you are seeking to meet.

HOW?   This question defines your overall strategy—how you will deliver the goods—and summarizes the driving forces to accomplish your vision.

The vision statement of Grace Fellowship Church in Baltimore is "to mobilize an army of men and women who love Christ with their whole being, who relate biblically in their circles of relationships, who maximize their unique giftedness and calling, in order to help fulfill the Great Commission by reaching unreached people around the world."

At this point, if you are an established church or religious organization, your key units also would contribute their mission statements.

Design a Strategic Ministry Model

THREE-TO-FIVE-YEAR FAITH GOALS.   Establish goals that are expressions of faith—what you believe God wants your church to be or become in the next three to five years. Describe the kinds of people your church will be reaching, the needs that are being met, and the growth that is occurring. Make your goals specific enough that someone could read them and then produce an accurate video presentation of your church in the future.

CRITICAL SUCCESS INDICATORS.   How will you know if your church is being effective? What measurements will you use to ensure you are fulfilling your congregation's God-given potential? Some of these measurements could include:

- Percentage of people involved in groups.
- Percentage of people using their spiritual gifts.
- Percentage of growth by conversion.
- Percentage of growth from stray sheep returned.
- Annual and decade growth rate.
- Giving levels per worship attender.
- Growth in Christian character and maturity (the most difficult to measure).

SPECIFIC GAME PLAN.   How will the proposed objectives be achieved? A strategic ministry model describes visually how your church intends to progress from where you are to where you want to be. You will need to clarify the various stages in your growth plan and the driving forces that will move you from stage to stage. For example, a church using a strategy of increasing its number of Sunday-school classes will need to document how unchurched people will be reached and assimilated, when and how new classes will be formed, and how the church will accommodate and finance the increasing number of people in terms of education, worship, and parking space. A church employing the strategic model of multiplying small groups through decentralized ministry (outlined in chapter 6) needs to answer similar questions, but will not have as exorbitant facilities costs (although housing is always a consideration in this step). Another important factor is identifying and training the expanding leadership team needed to carry out the ministry required.

As you shape your strategic ministry model, keep in mind that your design must be consistent with and build on your church's identified values and mission. But you also will need lots of free-wheeling discussion and interaction during this stage to maximize creative thinking. Remember that your strategic ministry model must be proactive so that you can move from where you are to where God wants your church to be.

Complete Reality Checks

The focused creativity of the strategic ministry modeling generates some stimulating goals. But now it's time to come back to earth! Is the model you are proposing realistic and achievable?

PERFORMANCE AUDIT.   Test your church's capability to achieve its goals. Measure your past performance in the key result areas identified during the strategic modeling phase. Look carefully at your church's resources (leadership, facilities, and so on). Do you have adequate resources to achieve what you are setting out to do? If things continued as they have for the past five years, would you accomplish your goals?

GAP ANALYSIS.   From your performance audit, you must identify gaps in your plan. For example, if your church has been growing at 3 percent per year for the past ten years, and you are projecting 30 percent annual growth for the next five years, what is significantly changing in your strategic approach in ministry that will increase your growth by a factor of ten? If your plan reflects business as usual, you don't have a strategic plan. You have a pipe dream.

ADJUST THE STRATEGIC MINISTRY MODEL.   Where needed, you will return to the previous phase and revise your strategic model until the gaps are manageable. Redesigning helps you ensure that your plan will become a reality. It is much better to have something fail on paper than in real life! Doing careful reality checks and making necessary adjustments increases your probability of success.

Don't forget that you'll need to check again the consistency of your proposed program with the congregational values and mission statement.

CONTINGENCY PLANNING.   Identify major opportunities and threats to the church, and indicators suggesting these opportunities or threats are likely to become realities (such as interest rates). Think through alternative plans. As Louis Pasteur said, "Chance favors the prepared mind."

Establish Action Plans

Now that you have a well-developed strategic ministry model addressing the overall approach to the next three to five years, it's time for specific action planning by all departments.

DEPARTMENTAL ACTION PLANNING. Each department in your church (worship, missions, children, youth, community outreach, and so on) needs to develop functional plans in order to achieve its goals. These are akin to the specialized game plans of sports teams. Each unit of the team has specific objectives to accomplish, which, if combined with the other units, result in a team victory. So each department or organizational unit in the church needs to design its own specialized game plan to help accomplish its overall goals. The basic questions *who, what, where, when, why, how,* and *how much* must be answered.

AGREEMENT TO SHARE RESOURCES. Here's where participatory management pays dividends. Because people at all levels have been represented and involved during every phase of the process, it will be far easier for the various departments or units in your church to agree to work together and share the limited available resources for the church's overall welfare. Even as differences arise, the strategic planning team brings together the key representatives from the various departments to work out the differences and gain consensus.

PUTTING IT ALL TOGETHER. Finally, the strategic planning team can combine all the specific action plans into a unified strategic plan that not only identifies the goals, but also the details of how those goals will be accomplished.

Implement Your Plan

This will occur when all the units experience activity on all levels that will result in the successful completion of the church's mission.

MONITOR RESULTS. Use the critical success indicators to monitor your progress. Reports to the governing board should be made in accordance with the proposed strategic plan, noting not only areas of performance *worse than expected* but also *better than expected* (churches usually report the former and neglect the latter).

MAKE MID-COURSE CORRECTIONS. It's normal and expected that you'll make adjustments in your approach to the ministry as needed. But because you have done such a thorough job in the planning process, your workers carrying out the ministry understand the overall values and objectives. Thus the strategic plan is a useful, working document that helps your members make week-to-week ministry decisions.

SCAN THE ENVIRONMENT. Throughout the process, continually survey and monitor the reality out there as well as inside the church. Discover

ideas you can borrow from others to make your church's ministry even
more effective. Tom Peters calls this "creative swiping":

> In today's ever accelerating business environment, you must put "NIH"
> ("Not Invented Here") behind you—and learn to copy (with unique
> adaptation/enhancement) from the best! Do so by aggressively seeking
> out the knowledge of competitors (small and overseas) and interesting
> noncompetitors. Become a "learning organization." Shuck your
> arrogance—"if it isn't our idea, it can't be that good"—and become a
> determined copycat/adapter/enhancer.

> The best leaders are the best note-takers, the best "askers," the best
> learners. They are shameless thieves.

> Note, however, that such creative swiping is by no means plain copying,
> which in a fast-moving work is increasingly useless. . . . Creative swip-
> ing, which amounts to adapting ideas from unconventional sources, aims
> solely at creating uniqueness.[12]

Action Steps

**Work with your governing board and key ministry leaders to clarify
each of the following issues:**
   What values do we consider essential for our ministry?
   What is the statement of mission for our church?
   What are the critical indicators for success in our church?

Identify any obstacles restricting your church's growth:
   Lack of clear ministry values
   Lack of intentional approach to ministry
   Lack of ownership
   Lack of excellence
   Lack of finances
   Lack of ministry space
   Organizational strangulation

**Decide upon and implement an annual goal setting and budgeting
process that maximizes involvement.**
   *The Pastor's Planning Workbooks are very helpful tools (available from
   Charles E. Fuller Institute).* See Leading and Managing Your
   Church *for discussion of obtaining ownership and planning work-
   sheets.*

What working ideas can we borrow from others for our ministry?

**Make word-of-mouth marketing a systematic process in getting
people in your church to support new ideas.**

Tom Peters stresses that people buy a product principally upon the perceptions of respected peers who already have purchased or tried the product. Service operations therefore must "use systematic word-of-mouth campaigns as the keystone for launching all new products and services. The campaign should include specific and detailed strategies to land a half-dozen progressive (probably not big) customers prior to full-bore roll-out."[12] Work the networks of opinion leaders in your church necessary to make word-of-mouth marketing of avenues for assimilation operate smoothly.

Read and apply Christopher Adsit's book *Personal Disciple-making* (San Bernardino, Calif.: Here's Life Publishers, 1988).

Notes

1. Tom Peters, *Thriving on Chaos* (New York: Alfred A. Knopf, 1987), p. 36.

2. Contact Charles E. Fuller Institute for Church Growth. P.O. Box 91990, Pasadena, CA 91109 or call 1(800)C-FULLER.

3. For an expanded discussion of this topic, please refer to the book I coauthored with Carl George, entitled *Leading and Managing Your Church* (Old Tappan, N.J.: Fleming Revell, 1987).

4. Peters, *Thriving on Chaos*. p. 64.

5. Ibid., p. 80.

6. Peters, *Thriving on Chaos*, p. 96.

7. Lyle Schaller, *44 Ways to Expand the Financial Base of Your Congregation* (Nashville, Tenn.: Abingdon Press, 1989).

8. Peters, *Thriving on Chaos*, p. 366.

9. J. W. Pfeiffer, L. D. Goodstein, and T. M. Nolan *Understanding Applied Strategic Planning: A Manager's Guide*, published by University Associates.

10. *See* J. William Pfeiffer, Leonard D. Goodstein, and Timothy M. Nolan, *Shaping Strategic Planning* (San Diego: University Associates, 1989). It is an excellent resource.

11. Peter Drucker, "The Non-Profits' Quite Revolution," *Wall Street Journal* (Sept. 8, 1988), p. 30.

12. Peters, *Thriving on Chaos*, pp. 228, 233, 234.

Principle 10

Starting Churches That Reproduce

Then Jesus came to them and said, "All authority in heaven and on earth has been given to me. Therefore go and make disciples of all nations, baptizing them in the name of the Father and of the Son and of the Holy Spirit, and teaching them to obey everything I have commanded you. And surely I will be with you always, to the very end of the age."

Matthew 28:18–20

Christ's assignment to the Church is clear. "Make disciples of all nations" "Nations" is translated from *ethnae*, or more literally, *people groups*, and addresses the cultural mandate. In order to be obedient to this command, we cannot rest until we have achieved the goal set before us of having a witness for Christ in each culture and subculture—in each people group.

As Luke records, Christ coupled this command with the statement: ". . . and you will be my witnesses in Jerusalem, and in all Judea and Samaria, and to the ends of the earth" (Acts 1:8). This final statement addresses the geographical mandate, to be witnesses:

- In Jerusalem (local).
- In Judea (surrounding region).
- In Samaria (nearby but culturally dissimilar).
- To the ends of the earth (worldwide).

The Book of Acts tells the story of the establishment, growth, and multiplication of the Church in *initial* and *partial* fulfillment of these commands:

- In Jerusalem (chapters 1 to 7).
- In Judea and Samaria (chapter 8).
- Toward the ends of the earth (chapters 9 to 28).

"Chapter 29" is what I like to consider the final chapter of this story—the fulfillment of the Great Commission. I pray and hope that our generation is the one which is writing the words of this chapter.

The twin passages of Matthew 28 and Acts 1 show that the focus of our church-planting efforts must be both *local* and *global*. Sometimes we tend to view our church-planting or missions process as an either/or. A church may focus all its energies on local evangelism and discipleship, thinking, "The world beyond is too big or too far away for us to worry about it." This was the error of the earliest church, whom God had to disburse through tribulations in order to get them to obey the to-the-ends-of-the-earth part of the command. The error of many contemporary churches is to ignore our neighbor but salve our consciences by designating our monies in support of missionaries in far away lands, thus thinking we have fulfilled our responsibility toward the Great Commission. (The American answer to every problem is to throw money at it and hope it goes away!)

The idea of fulfilling the Great Commission should not be simply a noble goal to which churches pay lip service once each year during missions conference week. Rather, fulfilling the Great Commission should be the focus of all that we do together as a church. Because it is a *Great* Commission it needs to pervade every level of our lives. Everything that we do and say as Christians and as churches should contribute in some way toward fulfilling that divine imperative.

Christ's own commission was to go to the cross and die in our place, redeeming us and restoring us to the Father. He went straightway, without turning to the left or to the right. Thank God that he did not turn aside from the task or delay, as we have done again and again throughout the past two millennia!

I do not own a dog, but always have been impressed by their loyalty. Jack London tells a story of a man whose dog was extremely loyal. To prove it to another, the man commanded his dog to jump off a high cliff. Without a moment's hesitation the dog leapt toward the abyss. At the last possible moment the man reached out and snatched the dog, saving it from the plunge. The dog, never doubting, wagged its tail and licked the man's face.

Throughout the Bible, we see a picture of a creation readily obedient to the commands of God; that is, all creation, except man. John 1:11 says, "He [Christ] came to that which was his own, but his own did not receive him." He came unto all creation, but only man did not receive him. The rest of creation willingly obeyed his commands. Balaam's ass turned aside from the angel of the Lord. God prepared the great fish to swallow Jonah. The ravens faithfully brought Elijah his food. Christ instructed the disciples to cast their nets to the right side of the boat, and an entire school of fish was waiting obediently. (Somehow I envision no stragglers!) Why, then, have people so often been recalcitrant to do God's will?

My prayer for my own life and for my church is that we become so accustomed to hearing and *immediately* doing God's will that it becomes second nature to us. I pray that we won't waste time sitting and weighing options and consequences, but instead would live thus: "God said it; I'm doing it."

Therefore obeying the Great Commission simply will not be something you do for whatever perceived benefit will come to your church. We unquestioningly must take up the task *simply because God commands it.*

Many have commended our church for planting six daughter churches in our eleven-year history. If I had to do it all over again, however, I now realize that God would have been more pleased with our *immediate* obedience to his command. We waited six years before planting our first daughter church. Now I see that it's possible and desirable for a new church to plant its first new church within a two- or three-year period. Doing this gives ownership to your church and accustoms its members to the seriousness of your goal to be a church-planting church.

You may have noticed that I jumped very quickly from the subject of fulfilling the Great Commission to the assumption that this means planting churches. Perhaps some readers might be left in the dust by such a transition. "I understand the importance of fulfilling the Great Commission. But what does this have to do with planting churches? Aren't there other ways of working to fulfill the Great Commission?"

Yes, there are other ways. Giving money to missions does contribute toward fulfilling the Great Commission. But there are no better ways than by planting new churches. Just as you work toward your most important goals with a unified strategy that operates on many fronts simultaneously, so fulfilling the Great Commission means a church will adopt a variety of approaches—supporting foreign missions endeavors, disciple making at home, holistic kingdom ministries, and most important, planting new churches. All work together to help fulfill the Great Commission.

Why Start New Churches?

Some of the reasons for starting new churches are very obvious. The body of Christ grows at an enhanced rate when it plants new churches.

The Nature of the Church

Effective disciple making requires that the members of the body of Christ work together, using their gifts to bring people into a personal relationship with Christ and then training them to obediently follow their new Master. The best context for this process of making disciples is the church—the local body of believers. Dr. David Hesselgrave remarks in his book, *Planting Churches Cross-Culturally:*

> So intimate is the relationship between Gospel proclamation and church-planting that they cannot be divorced without doing violence to the mission of the church. . . . The primary mission of the church and, therefore, of the churches is to proclaim the Gospel of Christ and gather believers into local churches where they can be built up in the faith and made effective in service, thereby planting new congregations throughout the world.[1]

Consider, for example, the apple tree. We normally consider the fruit of the apple tree to be the apple, but that is only part of the picture. The apple is merely a package of seeds intended to produce the ultimate fruit—more apple trees. The body of Christ is like the apple tree—producing individual disciples and more congregations.

The Historical Record

Christianity has always expanded through the multiplication of churches. The Book of Acts records how the boundaries of the Christian faith were pushed to the uttermost parts of the world through the multiplication of new churches. To this day, throughout every generation, Christianity has extended to new areas and new peoples via the multiplication of new churches. It is axiomatic that "the church is always only one generation away from extinction." You and I are Christians today because those who preceded us faithfully reproduced their churches through church planting!

The World Realities

The reality of a growing population requires the multiplication of new churches. World population has exceeded the 5 billion mark and is climbing rapidly. It is estimated that by the year 2000, somewhere between 6 and 7 billion people will inhabit this planet. In addition to sheer members, there are thousands of different people groups that need to be reached through cross-cultural church planting.

The Vitality of New Churches

New churches have a kind of life and vitality attractive to the unchurched person and often a necessary component for catalyzing that person's coming to Christ. Little in life is more exciting than the birth of a new baby. Such an event softens and energizes even the hardest countenances. Witness the transformation of otherwise normal people into cooing and *ga-ga-gooing* grandparents!

The Biblical Mandate

On top of all this is the fact that *we never will fulfill* the Great Commission without the multiplication of churches. The vast majority of places around the world don't have enough churches to do the job. I'm not talking about Outer Mongolia here, but about your own hometown. If you doubt this, you can test it for yourself.

To do this, identify the number of healthy evangelical churches in your area—the type of churches where God's Word is honored and people become disciples. Your area probably can be defined in the automotive society as within a twenty-minute drive. Add up the number of seats in these churches, and then double the figure (assuming that if every church in your area were to thrive it would be able to offer two worship services and thus reach twice as many people as its seating capacity).

Compare this figure with the population in the same area. Subtract the number of available spaces in the churches from the population, and you should have a very conservative estimate of the number of unchurched in your community. Divide this figure by 1,000 and you should have a rough estimate representing the number of new churches you need to start *today* in order simply to accommodate your community's existing population.

This figure does not take into account the population growth in your area nor the fact that a diversity of cultural people groups in your community would require a greater diversity of churches to meet their needs. We need to guard against *people blindness*, which is the danger of not seeing segments of society—even in our own backyards—that we cannot reach with the Gospel by today's methods.

Common Objections to Planting Churches

C. Peter Wagner shares three common objections frequently raised by well-meaning believers when confronted with the challenge of planting new churches.

1. Won't the effort to plant a new church drain valuable resources from our own church? Shouldn't we spend our energy helping our own church grow first? Starting a new church will indeed require valuable resources (of people, energy, time and funds), which might otherwise be used toward helping your own church grow. However, helping plant new churches is one of the healthiest and most natural tasks a church can do (even though the process usually doesn't occur naturally, without the mother church's intentionality). After CBC began planting churches, we became acutely aware of a principle we began to call "God's math."

God's math is what happens when you take seriously Christ's command: "Give, and it will be given to you. A good measure, pressed down, shaken together and running over, will be poured into your lap. For with the measure you use, it will be measured to you" (Luke 6:38). We usually interpret this passage as referring to stewardship of resources, although in context Christ was talking about forgiving others. But we discovered that the principle stretches across many boundaries.

In 1986 our third and most ambitious church-planting project was underway. As we progressed it soon became apparent that God was calling a large slice of our church to be a part of the project. This slice included about 100 people, including many key leaders, as well as much of our giving base. To release such a valuable slice of our body was a faith-stretching act, to say the least, and we worried what damage to our church might occur as a result. But we felt that God was calling us to generosity, and so we proceeded according to plan and said good-bye to those human and other resources God called to the new church.

A month or two later, we discovered something very surprising. Although we experienced a preliminary dip in attendance and giving, levels of both these indicators soon climbed back up to their usual place—and then quickly beyond. God honored our willingness to give sacrificially, just as he promised. "One man gives freely, yet gains even more; another withholds unduly, but comes to poverty. A generous man will prosper; he who refreshes others will himself be refreshed" (Proverbs 11:24, 25).

So it has gone each time since that we have released a daughter church. During the writing of this book CBC has released yet another. This one took 150 people, a number that included about 20 percent of the key lay leadership, including cell-group leaders, ministry leaders, and one of three professional pastors on the leadership team. CBC also contributed substantial financial support and other resources. As usual, the church braced for a temporary decline in the indicators the weekend after these people officially were released. Surprisingly, rather than dipping as expected, our indicators were *all up—the very next week after releasing 150 people!* Each week since, attendance and giving have climbed even higher. God has amazed CBC once again by his goodness. He is faithful to prove himself willing to bless us beyond all that we dare ask or think!

As I have consulted with churches I have begun to realize the universality of this phenomenon. A mother church willing to give of its own through planting a daughter church generally will experience that God replaces two people for each one of those whom he sends, usually within a year. Although the prime reason for this is spiritual— God honors his promise to bless our sacrificial giving—we also have discovered more tangible benefits.

One benefit is that reproducing a daughter church has a certain cleansing effect on a mother church. As a church matures it tends to accumulate a minority whose vision differs slightly from that of the church's core leadership. If allowed to remain for a long time, these people's attitudes eventually might deteriorate and cause a loss of momentum in the church.

The new church will be slightly different from the mother church. Two churches will reach more people than one. What many people don't realize is that two churches of 200 people will reach a far greater number of people than single larger church of 400 people. The idea is similar to that employed by shopping malls. Building many different types of stores together in one place will bring more customers and increase sales over the sum of what each of the stores could do if operating independently. Each church has a different personality and will attract new and different people. Thus we need *many different kinds of churches for many different kinds of people.*

In the first scenario, actual loss may occur to the kingdom of God because of the loss of momentum to your church. In the second, no net gain will occur, which is almost the same thing as a loss anyway.

In addition to having a cleansing effect, reproducing a daughter church increases your church's faith in God's faithful provision. The closer we live to the edge, the more likely we are to depend upon God to provide our needs. Beginning a new church has the very definite effect, at least for a short time, of giving your church a push near the edge.

But many churches use this realization as an excuse *not* to plant daughter churches. So often I've heard, "We're in a survival mode right now. We'll worry about church planting after we gain some momentum." Such churches don't realize they very well may *always* be in a survival mode. Gaining momentum results from obedience and sacrifice, rather than a stubborn maintenance mentality. A core biblical truth, practiced by so few church leaders and modeled by so few pastors, is that *God blesses giving and prospers the giver*.

Have you ever thought about why churches that have planted many daughter churches seem themselves to be flourishing? Don't confuse cause and effect here. You may look at such a church and think, "They became a great church, so they went out and planted new churches." In reality, the truth may be the reverse: In obedience to Christ, they went out and planted new churches.

2. Don't high start-up costs make planting a new church a more expensive way of reaching the unchurched? This is simply not true! Planting new churches is by far the most cost-effective means of evangelism. You will win more converts at a lower cost, through new churches rather than established congregations.

It is true indeed that planting a daughter church will cost something, and Christ advises us always to count the cost. He never advises us not to pay the cost, but simply to realize its implications.

3. We've built such wonderful, caring relationships at our church. Splitting up our fellowship would be like severing an arm!

Prospective mother churches also may be frightened by the prospect of breaking fellowship with those with whom they have developed caring relationships. (We noted in chapter 6 how this same unfounded fear often hinders cell groups from multiplying.) Our natural desires in this regard are contrary to the desires of the Holy Spirit, who always has led Christians forth from fellowship to move out in ministry.

> In the church at Antioch there were prophets and teachers: Barnabas, Simeon called Niger, Lucius of Cyrene, Manaen (who had been brought up with Herod the tetrarch) and Saul. While they were worshiping the Lord and fasting, the Holy Spirit said, "Set apart for me Barnabas and Saul for the work to which I have called them." So after they had fasted and prayed, they placed their hands on them and sent them off.
>
> Acts 13:1–3

This fear does not express faith in God that he is building the body of believers throughout the world and expanding our circles of relationships. True, we miss the people we have sent out with daughter churches (although we still maintain regular contact with them, and having sent them out in the ministry seems to make our fellowship together all the sweeter). Yet God has added two people for each one sent out and vastly expanded our networks of relationships. Rather than the small household we once were, we are in many ways now a large family filled with many children and grandchildren—a happy blessed household of God! Every empty nest family I know that has raised and released grown children to begin their own families experiences this same phenomenon. Yes, they miss their kids, but they realize that releasing them is natural and healthy, and that the quality of life somehow wouldn't be the same if they had clung to their kids and sought to prevent them from leaving the nest.

As Christians, it is a continually challenging exercise to learn to *see the world from God's perspective*. We are here on the earth for a very short period of time, and we have an incredibly urgent assignment. We'll have plenty of time to recline at his table in his kingdom and renew all those old friendships. How much more blessed if those friendships are multiplied to the ends of the earth as a result of our faithful commitment to be a *sending* church, a church-planting church!

Christ prayed for us specifically in John 17:20–23, when he said,

> My prayer is not for them [his apostles] alone. I pray also for those who will believe in me through their message [us!], that all of them may be one, Father, just as you are in me and I am in you. May they also be in us so that the world may believe that you have sent me. I have given them the glory that you gave me, that they may be one as we are one: I in them and you in me. May they be brought to complete unity to let the world know that you sent me and have loved them even as you have loved me.

Our unity, our sweet fellowship together, has a purpose in Christ's eyes, and that purpose is "to let the world know that you sent me and have loved them even as you have loved me." Fellowship that does not contribute to or fulfill this purpose is fellowship destined to wither—or be withered—like the fruitless fig tree cursed by Christ.

Working Together to Extend God's Kingdom Locally

My colleague, John Hayes, reports two significant worldwide trends that will impact the way local churches interact with sodalic ministries to extend God's kingdom across the globe.

The first is the internationalization of the world's cities. Not only are we experiencing massive urbanization throughout the world, the majority of the world's mega-cities are ethnically diverse. John comments, "World-class cities increasingly belong to the world, less to individual nations." World-class cities may represent the gate into otherwise insulated, even closed, countries, penetrating beyond the barrier of nationalism.

The second is the impoverishment of the world's peoples. Latest statistics from the World Bank reveal that twenty-one out of thirty-five of low-income developing countries now have a daily calorie supply that is less than 1965's. Roughly two-thirds of the world is poor by our standards.[2] Viv Grigg predicts that fully 25 percent of the world's people will live in destitute squatter's areas by the year 2000.

The church's responsibility lies in three major areas: feeding the hungry, providing urgently needed disaster relief, and engaging in long-term community development to help alleviate the conditions which feed the vicious circle of poverty.

In the great debate about the purpose and function of so-called parachurch ministries, the church often overlooks or ignores the potential of partnership with these sodalities. I am convinced the influence of the church can be maximized effectively and extended through cooperation with many of these specialized ministries on the following fronts:

Compassion Ministries

Christ mandated, in the Great Commission, the complete obedience of disciples to ". . . everything I have commanded you. . ." (Matthew 28:20). Christ defined his own mission on earth in the words of Isaiah the prophet: ". . . to preach good news to the poor . . . . to proclaim freedom for the prisoners and recovery of sight for the blind, to release the oppressed, to proclaim the year of the Lord's favor" (Luke 4:18, 19).

Later he spoke to his disciples:

> I have set you an example that you should do as I have done for you. I tell you the truth, no servant is greater than his master, nor is a messenger greater than the one who sent him. Now that you know these things, you will be blessed if you do them.
>
> John 13:15–17

> I tell you the truth, anyone who has faith in me will do what I have been doing. He will do even greater things than these, because I am going to the Father. And I will do whatever you ask in my name, so that the Son may bring glory to the Father. You may ask me for anything in my name, and I will do it.
>
> John 14:12–14

Compassion ministries exist in most areas that can assist a church in its desire to minister to:

- The poor and needy, hungry, homeless, and dispossessed.
- Prisoners.

- The sick and dying.
- Those who are hurting physically, mentally, or emotionally.

Church-Planting Ministries

Church planting is a mandate given to the Church at all levels—universal, local, and everything in between. Although church planting is a challenging task, many organizations exist which can help resource, equip and participate with local churches in that task.

Before you seek assistance you'll need to determine what kind of church-planting task you are seeking. If you are seeking to start a new church within your same cultural group, an organization like Church Resource Ministries can be of valuable assistance. CRM sends to cities catalytic or apostolic church-planting teams to work with established churches and denominations to plant new churches. CRM's ministry cuts across denominational lines. When we achieve our project goals, we very happily take our hands off and watch as the new church moves out on its own.

Perhaps you desire instead to plant a congregation designed to reach a different cultural group. This will require the help of specialists in missiology (cross-cultural work). In our local network of churches, we have such a specialist who has been a tireless strategist in the planting of Hispanic churches. For twenty years, Dr. George Patterson served as a missionary in Honduras, where he established a large network of churches and started a theological education and evangelism by extension training network which today is taking that Central American nation by storm.

Within your own denomination's missionary efforts, you may have such a resource person available to you. If not, a large number of missions agencies, as well as organizations like Pasadena's U.S. Center for World Mission, can be a great help in identifying and reaching "unreached" people groups.

You may need to consider committing funds and personnel to agencies that utilize bivocational church-planting teams. Lack of finances is not an obstacle to God; do not allow it to limit church-planting vision. I am aware of church planters who are moonlighting as window washers, bank tellers, caterers, janitors, and know of even one piano tuner! When structuring bivocational ministry some interesting and creative ministry opportunities arise. Christian businessmen sometimes find fulfillment in creating and filling positions specially designed to help support bivocational church planters. Remaining linked with networks of churches multiplies the options of how this may be done.

Key Ingredients to Planting Churches

The following Scripture passage provides a holistic image of the essence of the church-planting process:

> Jesus went through all the towns and villages, teaching in their synagogues, preaching the good news of the kingdom and healing every disease and sickness. When he saw the crowds, he had compassion on them, because they were harassed and helpless, like sheep without a shepherd. Then he said to his disciples, "The harvest is plentiful but the workers are few. Ask the Lord of the harvest, therefore, to send out workers into his harvest field."
>
> Matthew 9:35–38

Christ's words reveal three key ingredients in the church-planting process:

HOLISTIC MINISTRY. Christ's crucial ministry, even in its highly limited time frame and at its breakneck pace, still was holistically balanced. We see him teaching, preaching the Gospel, and healing "every disease and sickness" (v. 35).

COMPASSION FOR THE LOST. Christ's compassion arose from observation of and exposure to the lost. The manifestation of the crowd's *lostness* was its lack of direction and purpose. They needed Christ's spiritual leadership; they were "harassed and helpless, like sheep without a shepherd" (v. 36). How often do we take a walk in the real world and make the same observations of people all around us?

PRAYING FOR LEADERSHIP. Christ's response as a result of the compassion he experienced was God-focused and faith-motivated. "Ask the Lord of the harvest, therefore, to send out workers into his harvest field" (v. 38). What is needed to address the plight of the lost world around us is not new systems and better methods, but more workers equipped and sent by the Lord of the harvest.

Through Conservative Baptist Home Mission Society, CBC has long supported an indigenous Honduran missionary named Humberto Delarca. Humberto has proven to be what savvy shoppers might call "a darned fine buy." At a total support level of only about two thousand dollars per month (CBC supplies almost half of that amount), the young church planter has begun or catalyzed church after church after church. Now he has about ninety churches in his Honduran network.

Amazingly enough, even with these prolific results—or perhaps because of them—Humberto's network of churches has experienced threat after threat by Christians and Christian organizations. These threats could reduce the minimal level of support he now receives.

Humberto recognizes, though, that the battle is a spiritual one. I have no doubt that as a result of the time he spends pleading the cases of his churches before the Lord, God will continue to bless and multiply this very effective people movement.

Our task is to find such laborers, worth their weight in gold, who can maximize our investment. Humberto is one of these.

Church Planting Strategies

Your church can—and should—be a strategic player in the fulfillment of the Great Commission. Your people need to set their eyes on the world, just as Jesus directed when he told his disciples to begin in Jerusalem and go to the uttermost parts of the earth. Since the strategic starting point given in the Great Commission was the apostles' home area, and your strategic starting point will therefore be "your Jerusalem," when you devise your church-multiplication strategy you will first need to determine the boundaries of your home area.

Unless your Jerusalem is extremely small, there is probably a need for at least one more church in your local area. Undoubtedly many people will not or cannot be reached by existing churches because of limitations relating to style or physical capacity. So begin to think about your local disciple-making capacity by first establishing the need for new churches near home base.

Decide how your church will be involved in church-planting ministries. There are numerous ways to help start new churches.

Start a Daughter Church

The church where I served as founding pastor, in Alta Loma, California, grew to an average weekly attendance of 1,300 in eleven years and planted six other congregations. Some of these churches "hived" off people from the mother church to start; others were begun from "stratch" by the founding pastor. Much of what we learned is found in *How to Daughter a Growing and Reproducing Church,* available from the Fuller Institute of Church Growth and Evangelism in Pasadena, California.

Work With a Church-Planting Team

Another effective church-planting strategy is to join forces with a mission organization or denomination that will send in a team of catalytic church planters to work alongside local team members in the establishment of a church. Church Resource Ministries, with whom I am privileged to serve as vice-president for New Church Development, often utilizes this approach. Our ministry cuts across denominational lines and when we have achieved our goals for the project we very happily take our "hands off" and watch as the new church moves out on its own.

Many church planters have found *The Church Planting Workbook* and *The Church Planter's Checklist* to be helpful. You can order those from the Fuller Institute.

Worldwide Missions

Churches also should work hard to develop a comprehensive, results-oriented missions strategy. Such a strategy focuses resources upon missionaries and missions projects where healthy, reproducing churches are being started across cultural bounds.

In addition, you may want to invest resources in establishing church-planting missions organization. CRM has a church-planting team in Australia which has as its goal not only the planting of churches, but also the establishment of an indigenously led church-planting organization, similar to CRM, which will continue the work after our American staff's visas expire and the government requires us to pull out in four years.

It Will Happen With or Without You

Fuller Seminary's Bobby Clinton, an expert on leadership theory, tells the story of George Pitt, a young man who was born on Raratonga, one of the Cook Islands in the South Pacific. When George Pitt was seventeen, his family moved to New Zealand, and there he became entangled in the affairs of an urban motorcycle gang known as Highway 61. After five years, however George was confronted with the claims of Christ and underwent a dramatic conversion.

A few years later he and his wife, Christine, joined a Baptist church in Auckland. With only twenty members, the church was struggling for survival. George became active in ministry with the small congregation, and a year after he joined, they invited him—with no seminary training and precious little other experience—to become their pastor.

Under George's spiritually dynamic ministry—he is a man who is pioneering *power theology* through an extensive practice of prayer and fasting—the church finally began to grow. Soon 100 people were attending, and then 200. At this point, George became convinced that God was blessing his church for a reason and that reason was to plant new congregations throughout New Zealand. In the next two and one-half years the little Baptist church which once almost despaired of life reproduced six new daughter churches in six neighboring towns and cities. Now they are involved in eleven more such church-planting projects that also may result in new churches in the next few years.[3]

God is raising up men like George Pitt, Dion Roberts, Tom Nebel, and Dieter Zander all across the face of this planet. Serving on the cutting edge of ministry, they are among a generation of godly servants who are contributing in various ways to the writing of "the twenty-ninth chapter of Acts." They are writing the history of the body of Christ in these last days before the Great Commission is fulfilled and Christ returns to be reunited with his bride and complete the redemption of creation. Your name, too, could be on that list of godly servants.

So few healthy churches are involved in reproducing as the church is supposed to that sometimes pastors regard these churches as if something is wrong with them. As Watchman Nee might say, they are *normal* rather than *average*. But just as every Christian can and should live the *normal* Christian life, so a church can experience the cycle of life that God intended. This cycle includes investing itself in ministry for the sake of making more and better disciples, and reproducing its life work through planting new churches bearing the image of its passion to multiply the kingdom of God until the Great Commission is fulfilled.

Action Steps

Analyze your community through a church planter's eyes.

> *Complete a comprehensive demographic study that identifies the number of unchurched people and lists potential target groups.*
> *Look at your community through the holistic model used by CRM.*

Culturally:
   E-0   those within the culture of your church
   E-1   those outside your church but within essentially the same culture

E-2   those from a somewhat different culture
E-3   those from a radically different culture

Economically:
P-0   below poverty
P-1   working class
P-2   middle class
P-3   upper class

	P-0	P-1	P-2	P-3
E-0				
E-1				
E-2				
E-3				

As a result of your demographic study the percentage or amounts of population in your target area should be broken down and entered into each square on the grid. Once this task is completed, one balanced way to approach the task of fulfilling the Great Commission is to follow through and allocate your holistic church-planting resources in accordance with the percentages in each box. Using this method will cause your church to increase greatly its proportion of resources allocated to poverty or working-class peoples, usually found within the same or a nearby but different culture.

Allocate your finances appropriately.

For a church that is just getting started in this area of stewardship, you may wish to follow the holistic model developed by CRM: set aside 10 percent of your church's resources for missions, divided as follows:

- half to local missions
- half to global missions

Allocations in either half should approximate these percentages:

- E-1 = 25%
- E-2 and/or E-3 = 50%
- P-0 = 25%

You may wish to develop an alternate model that more closely aligns with your church's particular philosophy of ministry. It should represent your best attempt to approach allocation of ministry resources from a holistic viewpoint, keeping the balanced needs of a hurting humanity in perspective.

Focus your investing in people and sodalities in proportion to your missions priorities and goals.

Unleash your people for church-planting ministry.

Share the vision of church planting through consistent storytelling, biblical teaching, and inspiration.

Appoint a church-planting task force in order to investigate the feasibility of starting a daughter congregation.

Give high profile to the commissioning (the official release) of your people for compassion and church-planting ministries.

Invest in and work with like-minded sodalities to help your congregation start new churches locally and globally.

Notes

1. David Hesselgrave, *Planting Churches Cross-Culturally: A Guide for Home and Foreign Missions* (Grand Rapids, Mich.: Baker Book House, 1980), p.33.

2. *World Development Report 1988* (New York: Oxford Univ. Press, 1988), p. 4.

3. Bobby Clinton, "Fasting and Praying: Let's Get Serious About Church Growth!"

Appendix One:

CBC Newcomers' Class Outline

Session 1

Icebreaker Game (Meet People With Similarities)
Overview of Class Content and Policies
Lecture: "What on Earth Is the Church Supposed to Be Doing?" (examining CBC's purpose)
Care-Group Session: "Getting Acquainted"

Care-Group Guidelines
Icebreaker—Four Quaker Questions
Relational Bible Study—Luke 10:38–42

Homework:

Listen to Spiritual-Gifts Tape, Complete Outline
Bible Study and Outline on the Nature of Discipleship
Reading Materials on CBC Care Groups and Children's Ministry

Session 2

Lecture: "Worship at CBC"
Lecture: "To Be or Not to Be (Baptized)"
Care-Group Session: "Spiritual Beginnings"

Icebreaker—Wallet Scavenger Hunt
Relational Bible Study—Luke 5:1–11

Homework:

Listen to Second Spiritual-Gifts Tape and Complete Outline
Fill Out "Salvation Survey" (Probing Spiritual State)
Read These Materials:

A Biblical View of Baptism
Small Is Beautiful (About Care Groups)
The Book Above All Books (on Bible Study)
How to Read the Book of Books (on Bible Study)

Session 3

Lecture: "How to Consistently Experience a Growing and Vibrant Christian Life"

Care-Group Session: "Growing Through Trials"

Icebreaker—Pair up and Determine Common/Uncommon
Relational Bible Study—Mark 4:35–41

Homework:

Listen to Third Spiritual Gifts Tape and Complete Outline
Read These Materials:

Purpose Statement of Youth Ministry
Overview of Children's Ministry
Conversational Prayer
Our Family Tree (Determining Networks of Redemptive Relationships)
Membership at CBC

Session 4

Lecture: "Children's Bible Classes"
Lecture: "CBC's High School and Junior High Ministries"
Care-Group Session: "Asking and Receiving"

Icebreaker—"On-Spot Reporter"
Relational Bible Study—Luke 11:1–10

Homework:

Complete and Score Spiritual-Gifts Questionnaire
Complete Ministry Checklists
Complete CBC Membership Application (if Desired)

Read These Materials:

Tips on Cultivating Relationships—Neighborhood
Fifteen Health-Determining Principles
Church-Planting Fact Sheet

Listen to Tape: Salt-Shaker Evangelism

Session 5

Lecture: "Membership at CBC"
Lecture: "Sharing the Good News"
Care-Group Session: "Happiness Is . . ."

Icebreaker—Childhood and Daily Work Sharing Questions
Relational Bible Study—Matthew 5:3–10

Homework:

Listen to These Tapes:

How to Meditate on Scripture
Life After Kids

Read These Materials:

> Sharing My Story: Ideas for Writing Your Story and Testimony Evaluation

Write Out Personal Story (Detailed Outline Okay)
Read These Materials:

> How to Walk Through the Gospel
> Friendship Evangelism and Your Job
> You Are a Message
> How to Reach Your Extended Family

Session 6

Lecture: "Steps to Experience Financial Freedom"
Care-Group Session: "Becoming a Support Community"

Icebreaker—Stress Test
Relational Bible Study—John 13:1–5, 12–15

Homework:

Listen to These Tapes:

> Finding True Satisfaction—Financially
> Biblical Priorities for Money Management

Read These Materials:

> Four Priceless Gifts You Can Give Your Church
> Christian Stewardship
> What Did You Learn at Sunday School Anyway? (Helping Your Child Benefit Most From Bible Teaching)

Read the CBC Constitution and Write Down Any Comments or Questions
Complete Care-Group Information Form
Complete Newcomers' Class Evaluation Form

Session 7

Lecture: "Vision for CBC's Future"
Word Game—An Acrostic Describing CBC and Spelling Out Its Name
Graduation Banquet, Photograph
Homework Assignment Is Makeup Only

Appendices

Instructions on Preparing for Ministry-Involvement Appointment
Ministry Checklists
Membership Application and Responsibilities Sheet

Reprints of any of the materials listed in this outline are available at a small cost. For details, write:

> Community Baptist Church
> P.O. Box 490
> Alta Loma, CA 91701

Appendix Two:

Tracking and Assimilation Flow Chart

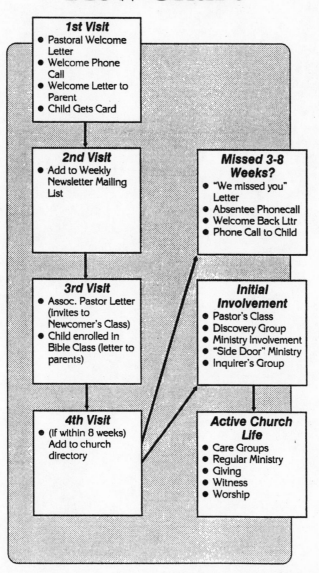

1st Visit
- Pastoral Welcome Letter
- Welcome Phone Call
- Welcome Letter to Parent
- Child Gets Card

2nd Visit
- Add to Weekly Newsletter Mailing List

Missed 3-8 Weeks?
- "We missed you" Letter
- Absentee Phonecall
- Welcome Back Lttr
- Phone Call to Child

3rd Visit
- Assoc. Pastor Letter (invites to Newcomer's Class)
- Child enrolled in Bible Class (letter to parents)

Initial Involvement
- Pastor's Class
- Discovery Group
- Ministry Involvement
- "Side Door" Ministry
- Inquirer's Group

4th Visit
- (If within 8 weeks) Add to church directory

Active Church Life
- Care Groups
- Regular Ministry
- Giving
- Witness
- Worship

Appendix Three:

Position Description: Cell-Group Leader

Position Summary: A cell-group leader (captain of ten) serves and encourages a growing group of people, who enjoy being together, so that the leader and all the group experience the Christian life together. A cell-group leader walks with God and takes responsibility to love and influence people so they progress from where they are to where God wants them to be.

Position Duties

1. Organize and lead regular cell-group meetings. Healthy cell groups (Acts 2:42–47) involve these essential ingredients:

   Teaching = learning and applying God's Word.

   Fellowship = building supportive, mutually accountable relationships.

   Worship = praising God for who he is and what he has done.

   Prayer = listening to and sharing intimately with God; interceding for others and God's work in the world.

   Power = experiencing the filling and outpouring of the Holy Spirit.

   Ministry = using spiritual gifts and loving each other in practical ways to meet needs.

   Evangelism = impacting our society and sharing the Good News so that people become Christ's disciples.

2. Provide pastoral care to all members of your group and their families as appropriate (visit in hospital, home, and so on).
3. Pray for all the people in your cell group each week.
4. Listen to the Holy Spirit on how he wants to work in and through the people in your group. The cell-group leader needs to ask, "How does the Holy Spirit want to release the unique gifts of people in this group?"
5. Train an apprentice leader who will branch off to begin his or her own cell group.
6. Be available to help baptize, lead communion, collect offering, and so on.
7. Be faithfully involved in ministry community.

Responsible to: the cell-group coordinator

Appendix Four:

Position Description: Cell-Group Coordinator

Position Summary: A cell-group coordinator (leader of fifty) is responsible for five cell-group leaders and their ministries. This includes the effective maintenance of the cell groups, pastoral care of their members, group growth and reproduction as well as the leaders' personal spiritual lives.

Position Duties

1. FACILITATE CARE-GROUP EFFECTIVENESS

    Help care-group leaders formulate goals and plans; monitor the implementation process. Encourage and affirm care-group effectiveness and growth.

    Attend each care group every third to sixth meeting and personally debrief with the leader.

    Help leaders discern group and individual needs. Ask probing questions to enable the leaders to identify priorities and determine next steps to be taken.

    Guide leaders to facilitate the use of spiritual gifts in their groups.

    Build team spirit through ministry-community meetings and prayer times together.

2. SHEPHERD CARE-GROUP LEADERS

    Pray consistently for each leader. Spend extended time in prayer to determine ministry-community huddle agenda.

    Build personal relationships with every care-group leader you supervise. Make regular contacts outside of the ministry community setting. Offer personal encouragement and/or guidance to each leader.

    Plan periodic planning times with your care-group leaders (at least quarterly).

    Follow up care-group leaders who miss ministry community, so that they receive the training and complete assignments on time.

3. CULTIVATE APPRENTICE LEADERS

    Help care-group leaders identify and invest in potential leaders.

Meet with potential care-group leaders and give vision for future ministry possibilities.

Invite them to care-group leaders' orientation meetings.

Follow up to enable apprentice leaders to launch their groups.

Identify with the care groups those with gifts and/or burdens for target-group ministries.

Multiply yourself by developing someone who can serve as a coordinator.

Responsible to: pastor

Appendix Five:

Gift-Related Job Descriptions

Sample Job Description   **ADULT MINISTRIES**

JOB TITLE: CARE-TEAM FOOD COORDINATOR

JOB SUMMARY: Respond to phone call from the church office about a new baby or hospitalization of someone in your worship service by:
(1) Calling the family to offer meals for certain number of days,
(2) then calling his or her team members to coordinate the schedule to prepare and take meals over

TIME COMMITMENT: As needs arise, but about one to two hours a month

LENGTH OF SERVICE: One year; renewable

WORKING RELATIONSHIPS: Responsible to care-team coordinator

QUALIFICATIONS: Gift of administration, mercy, leadership, service, or helps

LOCATION: Home

Sample Ministry Opportunities

Gift of Administration

Church-photographer coordinator: Receive assignments from staff, then arrange for a church photographer to cover.
People-Helper Trainer: Take new people helpers through a training process.

Project Mustard Seed commitment coordinator: Distribute visitation assignments to visitation team.

People-helper team leader: Distribute caring calls; disciple people helpers in a small-group setting.

Junior high activity sponsor: Help with youth activities by driving, bringing food, phone calling, and so on.

Senior high activity sponsor: Help with youth activities by driving, bringing food, phone calling, and so on.

Cell-group leader: Care for and lead a group of people in a weekly commitment.

Newcomers' class/spiritual-gift liaison: Schedule spiritual-gift appointments.

Newcomers' class host/hostess: Handle administrative details at a newcomers' class cycle.

Children's Bible-class teacher: Teach elementary children September-May or June-August.

Baptism coordinator: Run one baptism per month.

Sports-team administrative assistant: Assist sports coordinator.

Children's caring coordinator: Track newcomers and attendance so teachers can follow up.

Care-team food coordinator: Coordinate the scheduling of meals when needed for people in your worship service.

Tape-ministry helper: Distribute tape requests; receive tape orders.

Administrative assistant: Provide administrative help to the youth ministry in different areas as they need it.

Greeter coordinator: Coordinate the weekly greeters, info-booth people, substitutes, and so on.

Junior-department coordinator: Supervise and support the staff and program of fifth and sixth grades.

Middler-department coordinator: Supervise and support the staff and program of third and fouth grades.

Primary-department coordinator: Supervise and support the staff and program of first and second grades.

Nursery-toddler coordinator: Supervise and support the staff and program of the nursery.

Prekindergarten/kindergarten coordinator: Supervise and support the staff and program of four- and five-year-olds.

Preschool coordinator: Supervise and support and staff the program of two- and three-year-olds.

Children's Bible-class helper: Assist elementary teachers in working with children.

Early-childhood Bible-class helper: Assist early-childhood teachers in working with children.

Senior high school Son Village group leader: Lead a discussion group of six to eight students during the Sunday-morning class.

Junior high school Connection group leader: Lead a discussion group of six to eight students during one of the weekly Bible classes.

Discovery-group coordinator: Coordinate CBC's discovery groups by recruiting leaders and group members, and so on.

Gift of Evangelism

Sports-team administrative assistant: Assist sports coordinator.

Bridge builder: Provide regular phone contacts to newcomers to encourage them to enroll in Newcomers' class.

People helper: Caring for people in the church through shepherding and evangelism.

Greeter coordinator: Coordinate the weekly greeters, info-booth people, and so on.

New-resident contact person: Contact about ten new people a month to invite them to church.

New-marrieds contact person: Contact new marrieds in the community to invite them to church.

Outreach home discussion leader/host: Host or lead a home discussion for unchurched people for four to eight weeks.

Junior high activity sponsor: Help with youth activities by driving, bringing food, phone calling, and so on.

Senior high activity sponsor: Help with youth activities by driving, bringing food, phone calling, and so on.

Cell-group leader: Care for and lead a group of people in a weekly commitment.

Usher: Greet and seat worshipers; collect registration slips.

Sound technician: Set up and operate sound equipment for services and specials.

Awana leader: Discipleship of children through the weekly club time.

Awana helper: Works with Awana leader to disciple children.

Tape-ministry helper: Distribute tape requests; receive tape orders.

Children's Bible-class helper: Assist elementary teachers in working with children.

Early-childhood Bible-class helper: Assist early-childhood teachers in working with children.

Greeter: Weekly greet and orient people to CBC.

Phone-call greeter: Call newcomers after their second CBC visit, to welcome them.

Children's Bible-class teacher: Teach elementary-age children September-May or June-August.

Senior high school Son Village group leader: Lead a discussion group of six to eight students during the Sunday-morning class.

Junior high school connection group leader: Lead a discussion group of six to eight students during one of the weekly Bible classes.